EUCHARISTIC
ADORATION

"Msgr. Charles Murphy invites us to rediscover the riches of adoration."

Cardinal William Levada
Former Prefect of the Congregation for the Doctrine of the Faith

"Do not read this book: pray this book. An extraordinary combination of biblical study, knowledge of giants in the Catholic tradition, and profound spiritual insights borne, no doubt, of the author's own practice of Eucharistic adoration. An incomparable companion for one's experience of the worship of the Eucharist—invitational, poignant, and pastoral. Murphy draws us into appreciating what is never totally appreciated—the experience of 'communion' in and with the Eucharistic Lord. An excellent companion to anyone on the journey to deeper conversion and joy in the Eucharistic Lord."

Msgr. Kevin W. Irwin
Former Dean
School of Theology and Religious Studies
Catholic University of America

"Msgr. Murphy´s book calls forth a profound desire to gaze at the Eucharistic Heart and to sit at his school to become witnesses of his love."

Mother Adela Galindo, S.C.T.J.M.
Foundress
Servants of the Pierced Hearts of Jesus and Mary

"Using Jesus' last words and the virtuous qualities of Christian witnesses, Msgr. Murphy invites readers into a deeper relationship with our Eucharistic Lord. A great prayer resource!"

Rev. Kevin Russeau, C.S.C.
Novice Master
Congregation of Holy Cross

"What a wonderful gift! Msgr. Murphy's book will help everyone who reads it enter into deep, meaningful contemplation! I will recommend it to every parish where I speak on perpetual adoration."

Katie Pfeffer
CatholicAdoration.com

EUCHARISTIC ADORATION

Holy Hour

Meditations

on the

Seven Last Words

of

Christ

CHARLES M. MURPHY

Foreword by Cardinal William Levada

ave maria press AMP notre dame, indiana

Founded in 1865, Ave Maria Press is a ministry of the United States Province of Holy Cross.

www.avemariapress.com

Paperback: ISBN-10 1-59471-308-1 ISBN-13 978-1-59471-308-8

E-book: ISBN-10 1-59471-352-9 ISBN-13 978-1-59471-352-1

Cover image © Agnus Images

Cover by Brian Conley.

Text design by Katherine Robinson Coleman.

Printed and bound in the United States of America.

Library of Congress Cataloging-in-Publication Data
Murphy, Charles M.
 Eucharistic adoration : holy hour meditations on the seven last words of Christ / Charles M. Murphy.
     p. cm.
 Includes bibliographical references.
 ISBN 978-1-59471-308-8 (pbk.) -- ISBN 1-59471-308-1 (pbk.)
 1. Lord's Supper--Adoration--Meditations. 2. Jesus Christ--Seven last words--Meditations. I. Title.

BX2233.M87 2012
232.96'35--dc23

                              2012022137

For

Peter L. Gerety

Archbishop Emeritus of Newark

Mentor and Model of Priestly Virtue

on the occasion of his one hundredth birthday

CONTENTS

FOREWORD

When one thinks of adoration of the Eucharist, or Blessed Sacrament, one almost cannot help but conjure up the image of a quiet church: colored rays of gentle light streaming through stained-glass windows, the monstrance set atop the altar amid the flicker of candles, all inviting our contemplation and true resting in the Lord. One does not, on the other hand, think of the crowds of Hyde Park in central London! And yet, in his 2011 annual Christmas address to the Roman Curia, Pope Benedict XVI recalled this very image of tens of thousands of mostly young people gathered there in "eloquent silence" around the Eucharistic Lord. The witness of those young people reminds us that, in a world deafened by noise and saturated with lights other than that of the Gospel, it is *adoration* that stills us, attunes our hearts to the voice of God, and enlightens our eyes with the vision of charity. In the words of the Holy Father, adoration is the remedy for the "faith fatigue" so many Christians are experiencing today.

Surely, that prayer vigil of adoration and benediction of the Blessed Sacrament in Hyde Park in September 2009 stands as one of the more exceptional examples of eucharistic adoration in modern memory. But each and every moment of adoration is exceptional because of him whom we adore! Whenever we approach the Lord in adoration, we are in the presence of the risen Lord Jesus who loves us, heals us, and raises us up. We are confronted with the reality of love incarnate, not with some mere notion about God.

In these reflections on the seven last words of Christ developed for eucharistic adoration, Monsignor Charles Murphy invites us to rediscover the riches of adoration. These meditations are unique because of their setting. Like Hyde Park, the setting of Golgotha is anything but tranquil. In the Eucharist, Christ's dying and rising are present in mystery. In his presence we are invited to that emptying of self that roots our Christian life in humility before God and his mighty works—a humility that St. Paul hymned in his letter to the Philippians, urging us to "have the same mind that was in Christ Jesus, who . . . emptied himself" to take on "our human form" and "humbled himself and became obedient to the point of death, even death on a cross" (Phil 2:5–8).

As we listen to Jesus' words and contemplate his dying on the cross, we experience the power of his obedient love of his Father's will and purpose for him, a love that impels him to "empty" himself for us and for our salvation. We are spontaneously drawn to pray the refrain of the devotional Way of the Cross: "I adore you and bless you, O Lord, because by your holy cross you have redeemed the world."

May these meditations be for all of us a rediscovery of Christian joy in the "exaltation" of Jesus' rising and a source of renewal for us as we are buoyed up by the inner happiness and strength that arises from time spent in communion with God's tangible love for us. As society seems to move toward an ever more cynical view of faith and religion, surely the rediscovery of the great value of the prayer of adoration before Our Lord in the Blessed Sacrament will open minds and hearts to the compelling beauty of God's love for us. Thus can "faith fatigue" give way to lasting joy.

Cardinal William Levada
Vatican City
January 2012

ACKNOWLEDGMENTS

I am most grateful to Cardinal William Levada, prefect of the Congregation for the Doctrine of the Faith, for his generosity in supplying the foreword to this book.

The writing of this book was a delight for me, combining as it does reflections upon the passion of Christ and the adoration of its memorial in the Eucharist. I began the writing in the hospital, recovering from surgery. It was my small sharing in Christ's own sufferings. Surrounded by my books, I wrote the first pages in longhand supported by the hospital's bed table. Among those books were the two volumes by the eminent scripture scholar Raymond E. Brown, *The Death of the Messiah*, published in 1994. Father Brown lived with us at the North American College in Rome while he was doing much of his research. As he read every single scholarly commentary on every detail of the passion, which was his method, we would frequently ask him, "Where are you now, Ray, in the story?" I am indebted to him for his scholarship and most of all to the persons I name as witnesses beneath the cross, many of whom, as is obvious, I came to know personally.

INTRODUCTION

Gazing upon Our Eucharistic Lord

Pope John Paul II, in his encyclical on the Eucharist, sets forth as its underlying theme "the Church draws her life from the Eucharist." Christ promised to "remain with us always, until the end of time" (Mt 28:20), and that promise has been kept "with unique intensity" in the Eucharist. "Consequently," the pope continues, "the gaze of the Church is constantly turned to her Lord, present in the sacrament of the altar."[1] His purpose in writing this encyclical, he said, was to rekindle "this eucharistic amazement."[2]

The encyclical goes on to remark that "in many places adoration of the Blessed Sacrament is an important daily practice and becomes an inexhaustible source of holiness."[3] John Paul continues:

The worship of the Eucharist outside of the Mass is of inestimable value for the life of the Church....
It is the responsibility of pastors to encourage, also by personal witness, the practice of Eucharistic adoration, and exposition of the Blessed Sacrament in particular, as well as prayer of adoration before Christ present under the Eucharistic species.[4]

In the encyclical, John Paul alluded in a very personal way to his own prayer practice in recommending spending regular amounts of time in adoration of the Lord present in the Eucharist:

It is pleasant to spend time with him, to lie close to his breast like the beloved disciple (Jn 13:25) and to feel the infinite love present in his heart. If in our time Christians must be distinguished above all by the act of prayer, how can we not feel a renewed need to spend time in spiritual conversation, in silent adoration, in heartfelt love, before Christ present in the most holy sacrament? How often, dear brothers and sisters, have I experienced this, and drawn from it strength, consolation and support![5]

During my years in Rome as rector of the North American College, I often witnessed John Paul rapt in deep prayerful meditation before the Eucharist. I concelebrated Mass with him three times in the chapel of the papal apartments. We were allowed into the chapel at 6:30 a.m. for the Mass, which began at 7:00. John Paul had been kneeling on his prie-dieu since 6:00 a.m., his head often in his hand, in the center of the chapel, with no book, no rosary, and his eyes closed in contemplation. As pastor of several parishes over the years I encouraged the practice of eucharistic adoration. In one parish we introduced perpetual adoration of the Blessed Sacrament twenty-four hours a day, seven days a week. In a way that is hard to explain, the entire parish felt the power of this constant prayer going up to God from within our midst before our Eucharistic Lord. To my surprise, the most popular hours of adoration for each week were the so-called sacrifice hours in the middle of the night. I was told by some of those committed to these times that they looked forward with anticipation to this opportunity for silent prayer each week. Instead of becoming sleepy, they said, they became spiritually refreshed and energized by this time spent in the presence of the Lord.

The religious practice of spending a holy hour in the presence of the Blessed Sacrament is a personal response to the challenge Jesus posed to Peter and the apostles during his agony in the garden of Gethsemane the night before his death: "Simon, are you asleep? Had you not the strength to stay awake one hour? Stay awake and pray not to be put to the test. The spirit is willing enough, but human nature is weak" (Mk 14:37–38). The "agony" in which Jesus asked to be accompanied by prayer was the "terror and anguish" (Mk 14:34) Jesus experienced as he wrestled in a final confrontation with the powers of evil and darkness. "Agony" in Greek refers to an athletic contest, and this is how the evangelist describes Jesus' struggle in which his body emitted sweat "like drops of blood" (Lk 22:44) and from which Jesus ultimately emerges as victor. Icons of Christ the Pantocrator show a golden stripe on his right shoulder, the symbol of such athletic victory. Spending an hour with Jesus in prayer means to be awake to the eschatological meaning of Jesus' struggle and its consequences. The Eucharist is its sacramental representation.

The Church celebrates as its central mystery the Passover of Christ from death to life. This paschal mystery required that Christ shed his own blood for the salvation of the world, and this self-emptying is the model of what the life of every Christian should be. St. Paul, in his letter to the Romans, explains this fundamental "pattern" or paradigm of Christian existence:

> In my estimation, all that we suffer in the present time is nothing in comparison with the glory that is destined to be disclosed for us. . . . We are well aware that God works with those who love him, those who have been called according to his purpose, and turns everything to their good. He decided beforehand who were the ones destined to be molded to the pattern of his Son, so that he should be the eldest of many brothers."
> (Rom 8:18, 28–30)

Isak Dinesen, the author of *Out of Africa*, once wrote, "All sorrows can be borne if you put them into a story or tell a story about them." The story of our Christian existence is death and resurrection, a true dying without the possibility of returning to the past, and through that dying new life by the power of God, not just once, but over and over again.

In a special manner the seven last words of Christ each in its own way casts light upon this central truth of our faith. The Eucharist itself is the living memorial of the same paschal mystery as is manifest in the post-Resurrection appearance of the Lord to two discouraged former disciples leaving all behind in Jerusalem and making their way Easter Sunday to the village of Emmaus (Lk 24:13–35).

Jesus in his new existence is not recognized by the disciples as he joins them. He asks what they had been talking about, and one, speaking sarcastically out of his grief and disillusion, responds, "You must be the only person staying in Jerusalem who does not know the things that have been happening there these last few days." They then go on to speak of Jesus in the past tense as "a prophet powerful in action and speech" and how he had been crucified at the hands of the chief priests and leaders. Then, in a clear statement of their loss of faith, they said, "Our own hope had been that he would be the one to set Israel free." Their hope was not revived at the reports from women of his tomb empty and angels announcing he was alive.

Jesus, still a stranger to them, continues his walk with them and patiently, starting with Moses and the prophets, explained that the scriptures had foretold how the promised Christ had to suffer these things before entering into his glory. *Had* is the earliest explanation the first disciples could come up with for Jesus' dying and rising—it had to be that way. Later Paul would speak of the redemptive value of Christ's sufferings and how they took away the sins of the world.

Jesus agrees to the plea by the now intrigued disciples that he stay with them that evening. And, as it turns out, the way he stays is through the Eucharist. Notice the liturgical tone of the four verbs Luke uses to describe what happens next: Jesus at table "took" the bread, "said" the blessing, and then "broke" the bread and "handed" it to them. It was then that at last they recognized him before he disappeared. Hastening back to Jerusalem they reported to the apostles what had happened and "how they recognized him in the breaking of the bread."

The aim of this book is to be a worship aid for the time you spend in adoration and contemplation before the Blessed Sacrament. Each chapter begins with an exposition of the deep meaning of a "word" Jesus spoke from the cross. This is followed by the introduction of a witness to that word who in his or her life and teaching helps us to grasp more profoundly what Jesus was saying. I regard these modern persons to be part of the company who gathered beneath the cross with Mary, Jesus' mother. Each in his or her own way shared in the Cross of Christ, and each, we discover, was sustained and strengthened by his or her eucharistic devotion. Having meditated upon each "word" and pondered the saintly example of what it means during these holy hours, simply rest in the presence of the Lord and enjoy his company.

The composer Joseph Haydn, a devout Catholic, was given the daunting commission to provide musical interludes for a solemn reading of the seven last words of Christ in the cathedral of Cadiz in Spain. His work was first performed on Good Friday, 1787. At midday the doors of the cathedral were shut and the cathedral was enveloped in darkness except for a single light. The bishop mounted the pulpit to pronounce each "word" and deliver a meditation upon it. He then returned to the sanctuary and the congregation knelt while the sublime music of Haydn was played. Perhaps music more than words is best to probe the mysteries contained in these final words of Jesus.

To help in the dialogue with our Eucharistic Lord, at the end of each section I have provided suggested points for this personal conversation. They are intended to help you deepen your conversion to the Gospel way of life through your prayer. Some specific actions will be recommended, but mostly they will help you recognize how the mystery of the cross has entered your life and how you must carry that cross in imitation of our Lord.

The story is told of St. Jean Marie Vianney, the curé of Ars, that he observed a farmer every day hitching his wagon next to the parish church so that he could go in, sit, and pray before the Blessed Sacrament. One day the curé stopped him and asked what went on between him and the Lord during all these meetings. He replied, simply and honestly, "I look at him, and he looks at me."

"Prayer in my opinion," St. Teresa of Avila wrote, "is nothing else that a close sharing between friends; it means taking the time frequently to be alone with him who we know loves us."[6] May these meditations help you as you fix your own gaze upon the Lord in the Eucharist with total amazement.

At the conclusion of this book you will find a number of ancient hymns from the liturgy. They express the Church's deep piety regarding the events of the Passion and regarding the Eucharist. They deserve our reflection, over and over again.

How to Make a Holy Hour
Before the Blessed Sacrament

The Preparation *(kneeling)*

1. Enter now into the Eucharistic Presence. Focus your attention upon the One who is there with you. Take as much time as you need.

2. Use a prayer mantra to let the peace of Christ enter your soul. For example, you might use the "Maranatha" prayer from the Book of Revelation: "Come, Lord Jesus!" (Rv 22:20); or the familiar Jesus Prayer: "Lord Jesus Christ, Son of God, have mercy on me a sinner." Say this again. And again. Some pray the Rosary for the same purpose. Moving your fingers over the beads and repeating the prayers over and over have the same calming effect.

3. If there continues to be something preoccupying you, instead of trying to ignore it as a distraction, bring this also to prayer. Ask for the help you need. This prayer for help may be for someone other than yourself.

The Adoration *(sitting)*

1. Read the passage from scripture that you have chosen for your meditation. Read it several more times. Let its meaning sink in. You are now standing on Calvary beneath the cross of Jesus. He is speaking to you. You are responding to him with all your heart.

2. Stop reading. Let your mind roam over the spiritual expanses of the mystery of Jesus' dying and rising. Keep your eyes on Jesus in the Blessed Sacrament before you. Ponder how the paschal mystery has entered your life. Use, if you wish, the suggested dialogue points.

3. And now simply rest in the presence of the Lord. Enjoy his company, wordlessly. Let his peace and joy fill your heart.

4. Express the gratitude you feel for this privileged time. Ask God for the grace you need to implement your holy resolutions to carry the cross with Jesus more faithfully.

The Conclusion *(kneeling)*

Now is the time to say some of your favorite prayers. This should include above all the Lord's Prayer. According to ancient Christian tradition, the Lord's Prayer is recited at least three times a day, morning, noon, and night. Notice that the Lord's Prayer is composed of seven petitions, the first three centering upon God alone and the last four upon our relationship to him. It is the model of all prayer.

The Lord's Prayer concludes with words similar to these: "Lead us not to the test but deliver us from the evil one." This petition expresses what some have called the "nonheroic" element in Christianity. Jesus does not tell us to ask God to help us face any trial but, more humbly, to shield us from the power of evil that we acknowledge is more powerful than ourselves.

FIRST WORD

"My God, my God,
why have you forsaken me?"
(Mt 27:46)

St. Matthew reports these words of Jesus from the cross asking God why he has been forsaken. They were understandably most uncomfortable for the Christian community to recall. St. Luke substitutes another prayer, "Father, into your hands I commit my spirit" (Lk 23:46). In Luke, Jesus addresses God in the way we have become accustomed, "Father." In Matthew, Jesus says "My God," like any other human being. Matthew wants us to know that Jesus experienced death and abandonment on exactly the same terms as all of us, no secret trap doors, no escape hatches, and no exceptions. Some early Christian heretics even questioned whether Jesus actually died on Calvary or more appropriately only feigned his death. How could the Son of God die? But it is only through death and abandonment that Jesus could be our savior: he took all of us to the cross with him so that together we could in our common weakness and helplessness experience the power of God. As the Apostles' Creed laconically states, "He suffered under Pontius Pilate, was crucified, died and was buried."

When Jesus utters his lament, he expresses all the accumulated sorrows of the world, all the unrequited crimes ever committed, and all the deaths unpunished. Without turning away he faces the realities of sin, injustice, pain, and terror, and of evil itself. But Matthew wants us to remember that Jesus' lament was a cry not of despair but of prayer, the very first words of Psalm 22. His words are addressed to God who, though God appears silent, alone has the power to save when all human resources and solutions have proved inadequate and have given out.

The Book of Psalms is the prayer book of the Bible. The psalms were Jesus' own prayers throughout his life as a Jew. The psalms have been rightly called "a school of prayer" for they teach us how to pray.

The first thing the psalms have to teach us is that we do not have to wait to be in a pious mood or even especially religious in order to pray. We pray out of our actual situation at the time, good or bad, and this determines whether our prayer will take the form of praise or lament. We lay out our life before God as we see it at the time, and if our prayer is successful, we move from a subjective view of how things are to a more objective perspective, that of God. In the prayer of lament we may begin by expressing our feeling that no one can know what we are going through, that we are completely alone and cut off. Nothing and no one can help. But by the fact that we engage in the process of actually putting into words our situation and address them to God, even when God seems distant and uncaring, we place ourselves on the path to new understanding and living.

Psalm 22 that Jesus utters is a psalm of personal lamentation and desolation. It begins by describing with clinical honesty the present situation of the one who is praying as he sees it.

> My God, my God, why have you forsaken me?
> The words of my groaning do nothing to save me.
> My God, I call to you by day and you do not
> answer,
> at night but I feel no respite. (Ps 22:1–2)

The prayer then describes the self-loathing of one who feels unlucky and cursed.

> But I am a worm, not a man,
> scorn of mankind, contempt of the people,
> all who see me jeer at me,
> they sneer and wag their heads,
> "He trusted himself to God, let God[1] set him free!
> Let him deliver him, as he took such delight in
> him." (Ps 22:6–8)

The psalmist then gives in to his worst fears and most paranoid imaginings.

> Many bulls are encircling me,
> wild bulls of Bashan closing in on me.
> Lions ravening and roaring
> open their jaws at me. (Ps 22:11–12)

In complete meltdown, as if in a kind of psychotic episode, he feels he is going to die.

> My strength is trickling away,
> my bones are all disjointed,
> my heart has turned into wax,
> melting inside me.
> My mouth is dry as earthenware,
> my tongue sticks to my jaw.
> You lay me down in the dust of death.
> (Ps 22:14–15)

He lets his imagination run wild and imagines the worst.

A pack of dogs surrounds me,
a gang of villains is closing in on me
as if to hack off my hands and my feet.
I can count every one of my bones
while they look on and gloat;
they divided my garments among them
and cast lots for my clothing. (Ps 22:16–18)

Because of his brutal honesty about how desperate he is and how no human agency can help him, the psalmist now is in the right position to solicit divine help. He has arrived at the point of turning away from himself toward God.

God, do not hold aloof!
My strength, come quickly to my help,
rescue my soul from the sword,
the one life I have from the grasp of the dog!
Save me from the lion's mouth,
my poor life from the wild bulls' horns!
(Ps 22:19–21)

He has broken through his self-preoccupation. He can now focus upon God and be open to God's assistance. His isolation is also dissipating, and he invites his friends to join him in praising God. It was through this process of prayer that his lament has turned into praise.

I shall proclaim your name to my brothers,
praise you in full assembly:
You who fear Yahweh, praise him!

All the race of Jacob, honor him!
Revere him, all the race of Israel!
For he has not despised
nor disparaged the poverty of the poor,
he has not turned away his face,
but has listened to the cry for help. (Ps 22:24–26)

The letter to the Hebrews was a late addition to the Bible. Once ascribed to St. Paul and now, correctly, ascribed to an unknown author, perhaps a Jewish priest, the letter was considered by some to be too extreme in its description of Christ's humanity. St. Augustine, for one, loved it, and in its central section it provides a beautiful and fitting context in which to understand properly what Jesus was saying when he cried out from the cross, "My God, my God, why have you forsaken me?"

The letter to the Hebrews speaks of Jesus as a priest, a title never given him in his lifetime. The Jewish priests who carried out the worship of the Temple had to be members of a particular tribe. Jesus therefore could never be a priest in this sense. Jesus, according to Hebrews, is a priest "of the order of Melchizedek" (Heb 6:20).

The figure of Melchizedek appears in the Book of Genesis. He is the pagan priest to whom Abraham offers tithes and from whom he begs a blessing (Gn 14:17–18). Just as mysteriously as he appears in the biblical narrative, Melchizedek disappears, never to appear again. Following a rabbinical form of interpreting the scriptures that what is not described does not exist, Hebrews ascribes to Melchizedek a priesthood without beginning or end, an eternal priesthood (Heb 7:3). Jesus' priesthood, like that of Melchizedek, is eternal, it lasts forever. But according to Hebrews, Jesus' priesthood has other characteristics that uniquely suit him for this role.

> Since in Jesus, the Son of God, we have the su-
> preme high priest who has gone through the
> highest heaven, we must hold onto our profes-
> sion of faith. For the high priest we have is not
> incapable of feeling our human weakness with
> us, but has been put to the test in exactly the
> same way as ourselves, apart from sin. Let us,
> then, have no fear in approaching the throne of
> grace to receive mercy and to find grace when
> we are in need of help. (Heb 4:14–16)

In direct terms that some thought denied his divinity, the letter to the Hebrews describes how Jesus our high priest offered himself for our salvation.

> During his life on earth, he offered up prayer and
> entreaty, with loud cries and with tears, to the
> one who had the power to save him from death,
> and, winning a hearing by his reverence, he
> learned obedience, Son though he was, through
> his sufferings; when he had been perfected, he
> became for all who obey him the source of eter-
> nal salvation, and was acclaimed by God with
> the title of high priest of the order of Melchize-
> dek. (Heb 5:7–10)

It unsettles us to be told that Jesus our glorious high priest was reduced so low as to have to entreat God "with loud cries and tears" and that in order to win a hearing he had to demonstrate obedience. Furthermore, we are told he had to "learn" how to be obedient by his sufferings in order to achieve perfection. And yet this is what St. Matthew likewise teaches us in recording Jesus' cry from the cross, "My God, my God, why have you forsaken me?"

Dialogue Points for a Conversation with the Eucharistic Lord

1. Try to pay perfect attention now to the fact that the Lord Jesus is actually in this space with you. Let him speak to you and listen to what he says.

2. With total candor, let the Lord walk with you through the moments of your life when you felt the most abandoned and confused, past and present. Allow him to relieve you of these sorrows.

Simone Weil

(1909–1943)

The cry of desolation and abandonment of Jesus from the cross surely is one of the saddest verses in all of scripture. Another, and comparable to it, is a passage from the Book of Genesis, a book that begins with God's celebration of all his works as "good" and of the creation of the first human as "very good." But later, surveying the extent of human wickedness, God "regretted having made human beings on earth and was grieved at heart" (Gn 6:6). It was then that God decided to "rid the surface of the earth of human beings whom I have created" and everything else (Gn 6:7).

Simone Weil, the brilliant French philosopher and social activist, shared God's regret about the evils in the world and felt them profoundly and personally. Thus she could write, with dazzling insight, "God has emptied himself. This means that both the Creation and the Incarnation are included with the Passion." "Christ," she continues, "did not know this truth until he was on the Cross."[2]

Weil surveyed the world she knew in the horrible twentieth century, the most murderous in history, and concluded that God had to be absent for such evil to occur. She continues:

God is absent from the world, except in the existence in this world of those in whom his love is alive. Therefore they ought to be present in the world through compassion. Their compassion is the visible presence of God here below. Through compassion we can put the created, temporal part of a creature in communication with God. It is a marvel analogous to the act of creating itself.[3]

Traditional theology holds that God is omnipresent. But Weil dislikes what she calls the "abstractions" of theology and prefers to focus upon Jesus and his experience of God's absence from his sufferings. Though she consciously repudiated Judaism, she seems to be echoing here the rabbinic tradition found in the Kabbalah that refers to God's act of creation as *zimzum*: God's "withdrawing" into himself to create an empty place for something else to exist besides himself. Creation becomes more a divine absence than presence.

Weil once wrote in a notebook, "A single piece of bread given to a hungry man is enough to save a soul—if it is given in the right way."[4] In another place she commented, "Time is God's waiting as a beggar for our love."[5]

Simone Weil and her older brother, André, were born in Paris where they excelled in top-level schools. André went on to become a distinguished mathematician at the Institute for Advanced Studies in Princeton, New Jersey. In her years studying at the École Normale in Paris, Simone encountered Marxism and the plight of the working classes. After teaching for a while, she decided to experience firsthand the life of the factory worker and the farm hand. A pacifist, she traveled to Spain during the Spanish

Civil War. By the age of twenty-five, she "outgrew" politics and became drawn to religious belief. André once recalled when his sister received Leon Trotsky, the Marxist dissident, as a guest in her parents' apartment. After days of being challenged by Simone, he said to her, "I see you disagree with me in almost everything. Why do you put me up in your house? Do you belong to the Salvation Army?"[6]

Simone Weil lived in a period of political impasse and economic hardship much like our own today, but of even greater degree. Europe was going through a great depression, a world war was imminent, extremists of the left and right were gathering their forces, and Jews—even secular ones like Simone—were becoming targets. The lust for power ran rampant across the world stage. Government bureaucracy was eroding the rootedness of individuals and families and weakening the bonds of mutual caring. Religion no longer counted but was deemed a private affair, something done for an hour or so on Sundays.

More and more Simone felt drawn to Jesus, "who did not seek power, who surrendered, who prayed for his enemies, endured the aloneness, the scorn of everyone, even the betrayal of a close friend. He was naked to the end."[7] Simone in her *Spiritual Autobiography* states, "I never wondered whether Jesus was or was not the Incarnation of God, but in fact I was incapable of thinking of him without thinking of him as God."[8]

In 1938, Simone spent Holy Week and Easter at the Benedictine abbey of Solemnes. There she encountered another retreatant, a young Englishman, who shared with her a poem by George Herbert titled "Love." In her book, *Waiting for God*, she wrote,

> I learned it by heart. Often as the culmination of a violent headache, I made myself say it over, concentrating all my attention upon it. . . . Without knowing it, the recitation had the virtue of a prayer. It was during one of these recitations that, as I told you, Christ himself came down and took possession of me.[9]

Love

Love bade me welcome; yet my soul drew back,
Guilty of dust and sin.
But quick-eyed Love, observing me grow slack
From my first entrance in,
Drew nearer to me, sweetly questioning
If I lack'd anything.
"A guest," I answer'd, "worthy to be here":
Love said, "You shall be."
"I, unkind, ungrateful? Ah, my dear,
I cannot look on Thee."
Love took my hand and smiling did reply,
"Who made the eyes but I?"
"Truth, Lord; but I have marr'd them: let my shame
Go where it doth deserve."
"And know you not," says Love, "Who bore the blame?"

"My dear, then, I will serve."
"You must sit down," says Love, "and taste my
meat."
So I did sit and eat.

GEORGE HERBERT

In a meditation Simone wrote titled "The Father's
Silence," she pondered the words of Jesus from the cross,
"My God, my God, why have you forsaken me?" She
postulates a silent compassion passing from the Father to
the Son. It is the same compassion, she says, that should
prompt us to come to the aid of the destitute whom we
encounter.

> Before an afflicted man, this soul immediately
> responds with the true note. "My Father, why
> have you forsaken him?" And in the center of
> the soul the Father's silence replies.
> "Why has it been allowed that he should go
> hungry?" While one's thought is occupied by
> this question, one proceeds automatically to find
> bread for him.
> When the act is performed thus, the afflicted
> man is dispensed from gratitude because it is
> Christ who thanks.[10]

This, for me, is an example of the "new saintliness,"
of what Weil called the "unprecedented saintliness"
required in our times: to know the world's affliction, contemplate its reality, and then try to change it. The capacity
to give your attention, she claims, is rare and difficult;

in fact, it is a miracle. Weil defines prayer as "absolutely unmixed attention."[11]

In 1942, Simone and her family fled Europe for the safety of New York City. But Simone's solidarity with the poor and afflicted would not allow her to remain on the sidelines of this world conflict. She soon left for England to help in the French resistance. As her contribution to the cause of rebuilding France after the war, she wrote there her political masterpiece, *The Need for Roots*. She reduced her eating to the rations allowed to her countrymen during the occupation. Her health continued to deteriorate. On August 24, 1943, she died of starvation and tuberculosis.

Lover of the crucified and abandoned Christ and of the afflicted of the world, Simone Weil with her critical mind found that she could not receive Baptism herself, though she urged others to do so. She remained all her brief life a pilgrim, a pilgrim of the Absolute.

Further on in her reflection "The Father's Silence," Simone speaks about

> God dwelling in food. Lamb. In matter worked
> by human labor, bread, wine. That ought to be
> the center of peasant life. By his labor, if he so
> intends it, the peasant gives a little of his flesh so
> that it may become the flesh of Christ. He should
> be a consecrated man. Sanctity is a transmuta-
> tion like the Eucharist.[12]

Simone Weil wished her life to be a sacrificial offering in union with the Eucharist of Christ.

Dialogue Points for a Conversation with the Eucharistic Lord

1. Simone Weil has said, "Time is God's waiting as a beggar for our love." Since God has loved us so much that he gave us his only Son who for our sake accepted death, even death on a cross, ask Jesus to help you appreciate even more deeply how much you are loved, loved not for anything you do but just for yourself.

2. Ask the Lord to increase the space of your love so that you may share in his compassion for every single person. Ask him to help you pay greater attention to the people in your life and how you are part of them.

Prayer

> Lord Jesus Christ, present in the Eucharist, for me and for the many, unworthy though I am, help me to accept your invitation to "take this and eat of it," so that I may share the love I have received with all the afflicted ones I know. Help me to take to heart these words of St. Teresa of Avila:
>
>> Christ has no body now, but yours, no hands, no feet on earth but yours. Yours are the eyes through which Christ looks with compassion upon the world. Yours are the feet with which Christ walks to

do good. Yours are the hands with which Christ blesses the world.

Let nothing trouble you, let nothing frighten you. All things are passing; only God remains. Patience obtains all things. He who possesses God lacks nothing. God alone suffices.

SECOND
WORD

"Father, forgive them,
for they know not what they do."
(Lk 23:32–34)

This prayer of Jesus from the cross is unique to Luke's gospel, and many manuscripts of that gospel omit it. Perhaps Jesus' plea for forgiveness for those who were taking away his life seemed too much for the copyists. In the Acts of the Apostles, St. Luke has Stephen, the first martyr, utter a similar prayer: "Lord, do not hold this sin against them" (Acts 7:60).

It should not surprise us that Jesus would utter as a last word from the cross a plea for forgiveness of his enemies. In fact, no other world religion besides Christianity has made forgiveness so central to its belief and practice. Hannah Arendt, the eminent social philosopher, states very directly, "The discoverer of the role of forgiveness in the realm of human affairs was Jesus of Nazareth."[1]

According to Arendt, Jesus asserts that, not only does God have the power to forgive, but we too have this power (Mt 9:4–6). She declares it is only when we have forgiven each other that we ourselves will be forgiven by God. If we do not forgive from our hearts, neither will God forgive us (cf. Mt 18:35). It is as if God's power to forgive is held back unless we are willing to forgive. In the Lord's Prayer, for instance, we pray, "Forgive us our trespasses *as* we forgive those who trespass against us" (cf. Mt 6:12). In the act of our forgiving each other, God forgives. Arendt continues,

> The reason for Jesus' insistence on a duty to forgive is clearly "for they know not what they do" and it does not apply to the extremity of crime and willed evil, for then it would not have been necessary to teach: "And if your brother does

something wrong, rebuke him, and if he is sorry, forgive him. And if he wrongs you seven times a day and seven times comes back to you and says, 'I am sorry,' you must forgive him" (Lk 17:3–4). Crime and willed evil are rare, even rarer perhaps than good deeds; according to Jesus, they will be taken care of by God in the Last Judgment.[2]

Arendt contrasts forgiveness with its opposite, vengeance. Vengeance creates a chain reaction of unhindered retribution. Forgiveness frees us from merely reacting and creates the possibility of something new. Forgiveness furthermore is prompted by love for transgressors who are seen in their true self and not defined by what they have done, provided they change and repent (which literally means "retrace one's steps").

"Forgiving and the relationship it establishes is always an eminently personal . . . affair in which what was done is forgiven for the sake of who did it," Arendt explains.[3] This too was clearly recognized by Jesus who said, regarding the woman known to be a sinner, "For this reason, I tell you, her sins, many as they are, have been forgiven her, because she has shown such great love. It is someone who is forgiven little who shows little love" (Lk 7:47–48).

St. Luke's gospel is preeminently the gospel of forgiveness. It is this gospel that gave us Jesus' cry from the cross, "Father, forgive them, for they know not what they do." The compassionate Father does not merely wait for the lost to come to him: according to Luke, the

Father seeks them even before they seek him: the lost sheep, the lost coin, and the lost son (Lk 15:1–31). Unlike our usual way of thinking that repentance must precede forgiveness, Jesus' proclamation that sins are forgiven is what prompted sinners to approach him in the first place; knowing they were already forgiven allowed them to repent.

Scripture scholars speculate that the story of the woman caught in adultery and brought to Jesus before she was to be stoned in accordance with Mosaic law, now found in St. John's gospel (Jn 8:3–11), was perhaps first in Luke but was removed by the copyists as too shocking. Jesus seemed to be giving approval to adulterous behavior: "Let the one among you who is guiltless be the first to throw a stone at her" (Jn 8:7). The story then found its place in John where it interrupts the appearance of Jesus teaching at the Temple. In any case, it is apparent that God's forgiveness is lavish and limitless and, for some, can even seem scandalous.

On a recent visit to the Holy Land, I led a group of fellow pilgrims in procession along the Via Dolorosa in Jerusalem. Along the way we encountered four young boys and a donkey: one was riding on top, one was pulling on the rope ahead, and the other two were tormenting the poor animal, one by a whip and the other by shoving its haunches. The donkey's ears were raised in panic, but it uttered no sound. All I could think of was that the donkey somehow resembled Jesus and his tormentors who "knew not what they were doing."

Dialogue Points for a Conversation with the Eucharistic Lord

1. Peter asked the Lord to be specific about how many times we are expected to forgive another—say, seven times? Jesus replied, "Not seven times, but seventy-seven times" (Mt 18:21), that is, without any limit whatsoever. Ask Jesus to give you a forgiving heart.

2. Martin Luther King Jr. often spoke about the strength it takes to love as opposed simply to retaliating in kind. One theological explanation of the meaning of redemption and how it works is that we are willing like Christ to absorb the evil that is done to us and thus not add to the quantity of evil in the world. Pray that the Lord may help you to perform this redemptive task along with him.

WITNESS:
St. Teresa
Blessed by the Cross
(Edith Stein)
(1891–1942)

Hannah Arendt and Edith Stein were philosophy students in Germany before World War I. Arendt studied with Martin Heidegger, Stein with Edmund Husserl. Though Jewish, both women were strongly attracted to Christianity. Arendt wrote her doctoral dissertation on St. Augustine's concept of love, and Stein wrote hers on the idea of empathy. Arendt eventually made her way to the United States and had a distinguished academic career. Her five-part article, "Eichmann in Jerusalem: A Report on the Banality of Evil," written for the *New Yorker* magazine in 1963, caused great controversy.

After some years as a Catholic, Stein was finally allowed to enter the Carmelite Order in Cologne where she took as her religious name Sister Teresa Blessed by the Cross. Her clothing as a religious took place on April 15, 1934. Her spirituality was thus shaped from the beginning by the Cross of Christ whose shadow was then falling upon Germany and the Jewish people in particular. Edith Stein, with her sister Rosa, was to die in the gas chambers at Auschwitz on August 9, 1942. When they were arrested in Holland where they had gone to escape,

Edith said to her sister, "Come, Rosa, we are going for our people."[4]

Some years after she joined the Carmelites, Edith explained to another religious the personal significance of her religious name.

> I must tell you that I already brought my religious name with me into the house as a postulant. I received it exactly as I requested it. By the cross I understand the destiny of God's people which, even at that time, began to announce itself. I thought that those who recognized it as the cross of Christ had to take it upon themselves in the name of all. Certainly, today, I know more of what it means to be wedded to the Lord in the sign of the cross. Of course, one can never comprehend it, for it is a mystery.[5]

As a Catholic contemplative nun, Edith Stein maintained close contact with her family, even though relations were strained, especially with her mother. In a letter dated October 31, 1938, Edith confided to her mother superior worries about the family. She asked if Rosa could be allowed to leave home in Breslau for the safety of the convent in Cologne. "There is no longer any sense in saving money," she writes, "since they have to turn everything in when they emigrate. If only they knew where to go!" She continues:

> And I trust in the Lord's having accepted my life for all of them. I keep having to think of Queen Esther who was taken from among her people precisely that she might represent them before

the King. I am a very poor and powerless little Esther, but the King who chose me is infinitely great and merciful. This is such a great comfort.[6]

On the day of Edith Stein's beatification by Pope John Paul II in Cologne, May 1, 1987, the passage from the Book of Esther that Edith referred to was read at the Mass.

Back in 1933, Edith had written a letter that was personally handed to Pope Pius XI by her confessor. In it she begged that he issue a condemnation of anti-Semitism. A draft of such an encyclical prepared for the pope by the American Jesuit John La Farge has recently surfaced, but the encyclical was never issued.

At Christmas 1932, Stein reflected upon how the mystery of the cross is played out in the lives of those who belong to him for the salvation of the world.

> There is a vocation to suffer with Christ and thereby to cooperate with him in his work of salvation. When we are united with the Lord, we are members of the mystical body of Christ: Christ lives in his members and continues to suffer in them. And the suffering borne in union with the Lord is his suffering, incorporated in the great work of salvation and fruitful therein. That is the fundamental premise of all religious life, above all in the life of Carmel, to stand proxy for sinners through voluntary and joyous suffering, and to cooperate in the salvation of humankind.[7]

In 1943, while World War II was raging, Pope Pius XII issued his seminal encyclical letter on the Mystical Body of Christ. The Church, according to Pius, is more than a mere human institution—it is something mystical and transcendent, Christ's own presence in the world. This high and noble vision of the Church helped Edith Stein, and countless others, to remain faithful to the Church even when many of its members were complicit in the Nazi regime.

By Easter 1933, because of her Jewish ancestry, Edith Stein had been terminated from her teaching position at the Catholic pedagogical institute in Munster. She wrote at the time,

> I consider it an educator's duty to live through these times with the children. This includes making the effort to form one's own judgment, measuring the "movement" National Socialist (Nazi) against our own standards. . . . My lecturing was terminated at Easter. Do not be sad about that. Something more beautiful will be replacing it. What that is I am still unable to tell you today.[8]

As conditions in Germany deteriorated, Edith and her sister no longer felt safe in Cologne. They applied for asylum at a Carmelite convent in Switzerland, but when that fell through they fled to a convent in Echt where they resided between 1938 and 1942.

In a letter written in April 1939, Stein summarized her attitude toward her new situation.

My basic attitude since I have been here is one of gratitude—grateful that I may be here and that the house is as it is. At the same time I always have a lively awareness that we do not have a lasting city here. I have no other desire than that God's will be done in me and through me. It is up to him how long he leaves me here and what is to come then. *In manibus tuis, sortae meae* ["My days are in your hands" (Ps 31:15)]. There everything is well cared for. I need not worry about anything. But much prayer is necessary in order to remain faithful in all situations. Especially we must pray for those who have heavier burdens to carry than I have and who are not so rooted in the Eternal. Therefore I am sincerely grateful to all who help.[9]

As a kind of spiritual testament as she sensed her life drawing to its close, Edith Stein summarized her life's intention in these words written on June 9, 1939,

Even now I accept the death that God has prepared for me in complete submission and with joy as being his most holy will for me. I ask the Lord to accept my life and my death so that the Lord will be accepted by his People and that his Kingdom may come in glory, for the salvation of Germany and the peace of the world.[10]

On October 11, 1998, Sister Teresa Blessed by the Cross was canonized a saint by Pope John Paul II under the title of martyr and was declared copatroness of Europe. Her feast day, to be observed by the universal Church, was established for August 9.

After Pope Benedict XVI visited Auschwitz in May 2006, he reflected upon the experience in a general audience in Rome: "In the face of the horror of Auschwitz, there is no other response than the cross of Christ. Love descended to the very depths of the abyss of evil to save man."[11]

Edith Stein also recognized the new kind of saintliness that Simone Weil spoke about, a saintliness vitally connected with the struggles of the actual world in which we live.

> Immediately before and for a good while after my conversion, I was of the opinion that to lead a religious life meant one had to give up all that was secular and to live totally immersed in thoughts of the Divine. But gradually I realized that something else is asked of us in this world and that, even in the contemplative life, one may not sever the connection with the world. I even believe that the deeper one is drawn into God, the more one must "go out of oneself": that is, one must go to the world in order to carry the divine life into it.[12]

Along very similar lines the martyred Lutheran pastor Dietrich Bonhoeffer advocated what he termed "a new kind of monasticism," that is, not a flight from the world but getting your hands dirty trying to change it. He put it this way: "Only the person who cries out for the Jews may sing Gregorian chants."[13]

Dialogue Points for a Conversation with the Eucharistic Lord

1. Jesus asked for forgiveness of his persecutors, as did St. Stephen after him, because their persecutors did not know what they were doing. Edith Stein loved the German people and would not allow even the Holocaust to change her affections. How can you help your own acquaintances to discover their true selves apart from any wrong they may have done you or anyone else?

2. Edith Stein said we can only gain knowledge of the cross by experiencing it personally. In your time in the presence of the Lord, ask him to walk with you through those personal experiences you have had of the cross in your life and allow him to give you his peace.

Prayer

O God, my compassionate and loving Father, your daughter Sister Teresa finally understood her destiny beneath the cross of your Son, what it meant to be the bride of Christ under the sign of the cross. Help me to shoulder my particular sharing in Christ's cross and sustain me on my way with the bread of the Eucharist.

The Divine Praises

Blessed be God.

Blessed be his holy Name.

Blessed be Jesus Christ true God and true man.

Blessed be the Name of Jesus.

Blessed be his most Sacred Heart.

Blessed be his most Precious Blood.

Blessed be Jesus in the holy sacrament of the altar.

Blessed be the Holy Spirit, the Paraclete.

Blessed be the great Mother of God, Mary most holy.

Blessed be her holy and immaculate conception.

Blessed be her glorious assumption.

Blessed be the name of Mary, Virgin and Mother.

Blessed be St. Joseph her most chaste spouse.

Blessed be God in his angels and in his saints.

THIRD
WORD

"Today you will be with me
in paradise."
(Lk 23:43)

❧❖❧❖❧❖❧❖❧❖❧

The brief conversation between Jesus and the criminal who converted from his sins is like the Gospel in miniature. Unlike any other place in all the scriptures, here Jesus is addressed simply by his name, without any title: "Jesus, remember me when you come into your kingdom." Jesus responds, "In truth I tell you, today you will be with me in paradise." The Gospel of forgiveness has been preached to the very end, even from the cross.

Execution by crucifixion was commonplace just outside the walls of Jerusalem. The central posts remained in place so that the condemned could be nailed to a crossbar and hoisted up upon them. It was intended to be a most cruel form of death and humiliation, the condemned naked and exposed to the scorn of the public. Death took a while, either by asphyxiation or by simple loss of blood. As a Roman citizen, unlike Jesus, St. Paul was spared this form of execution and was beheaded. It is truly remarkable that the cross, an instrument of torture, has become the universal symbol of redemption through love.

St. Luke chronicles in a deliberate way the downward path of Jesus' accusers: first the religious authorities, then the Roman soldiers, and finally the criminals. In their accusations against Jesus they use titles that actually fit him: Christ of God, God's chosen one, and the Messiah. It is they who fail to understand that, because Jesus is all of these, he must die.

In the Acts of the Apostles, St. Luke has Peter declare about Jesus before the Sanhedrin, "Only in him is there salvation, for of all the names in the world given to men, this is the only one by which we can be saved" (Acts 4:12).

The sacred name of Jesus has unique power. Just saying it can cause demons to disperse. The repentant criminal invoked this name and was immediately forgiven.

It is entirely appropriate for Jesus to die in the company of ordinary criminals for he was known during his entire life to associate with sinners and even to dine with them (Lk 15:2). He constantly reached out to the excluded, the outcasts, and those labeled unclean and restored them to a place in society. The forgiven criminal was most likely a Gentile to whom Jesus also offered forgiveness and reconciliation.

Jesus used the word "today." Salvation begins the moment Jesus accepts his divine mission to die for the sins of humanity. The kingdom of God is inaugurated, the arrogant and the proud are put down from their thrones, and the little ones have the Gospel preached to them. In an instant, one who was a criminal is made Jesus' disciple—one who is "with Jesus," which in Christian terms is its very definition. Jesus told his disciples, "You are the men who have stood by me faithfully in my trials; and now I confer a kingdom on you, just as the Father conferred one on me: you will eat and drink at my table in my kingdom, and you will sit on thrones to judge the twelve tribes of Israel" (Lk 22:28–30).

Jesus astonished many by his power to release people from their sins (Lk 7:49). Raymond Brown, the eminent scripture scholar, has commented about the absolution the criminal was given on the cross: "Frequently called the episode of the 'good thief,' this is rather another aspect of the good Jesus."[1]

The invocation of paradise lets us glimpse the momentous nature of what is taking place. The tree of the cross now becomes the tree of life of the original paradise from which the first humans were expelled because of their disobedience. Christ is the new Adam who reopens the path to salvation for all the suffering people of the world. The cross itself introduces us to paradise. As St. Catherine of Siena said, "All the way to heaven is heaven, for Jesus said, 'I am the way.'"

Dialogue Points for a Conversation with the Eucharistic Lord

1. Conversion is the never-ending process of turning away from sin and toward God, a process that will not end until the day we die. We all have reason to say, "Be patient with me. God is not finished with me yet." God's mercy is available to us even up to the last moment of our life. With God all things are possible. Ask the Lord Jesus to help you deepen your conversion through his merciful love.

2. In very concrete ways all of us are called to carry the cross with Jesus. Try to see meaning in these trials as part of the royal road to paradise.

WITNESS:

Dorothy Day
(1897–1980)

Dorothy Day, with the French exile Peter Maurin, founded the Catholic Worker movement with its houses of hospitality for feeding and sheltering the poor and homeless. They also began a monthly newspaper, *The Catholic Worker*, to communicate the Church's social teachings. *The Catholic Worker*, true to its mission, still sells for a penny a copy. Day and Maurin preached and practiced a "radical" Catholicism of social justice, charity, and pacifism—radical in the sense of going to the roots of our beliefs and living out the consequences. Voluntary poverty and direct, one-on-one love of the poor are expected of all members. Dorothy always credited to Peter her discovery of this challenging vision of Christian personalism.

To humanize the slums through direct personal action was part of their vision. Another part was to establish agrarian cooperative communities, places that were an alternative to what Maurin called the lopsided money economy that robbed people of their most sublime instincts to use their heads, hearts, and hands as gifts to others. Through these direct personal actions he hoped to create a society from the bottom up in which it is easier to be good.[2] Pope Benedict XVI used similar terms in his social encyclical *Caritas in veritate* (issued in 2009), speaking of the need for "quotas of giftedness and community" to build up the bonds of community.[3]

It was never easy to live in a house of hospitality. Peter Maurin used to sleep with his trousers rolled up as a pillow so no one would steal them during the night. Stanley Vishnewski, a lifelong Catholic worker, commented, "The Catholic Worker is made up of saints and martyrs. You have to be a martyr to put up with the saints."[4]

I was only two years ordained when I met Dorothy Day in June 1964. A local Catholic college was hosting a two-day conference on civil rights that featured Dorothy Day and Martin Luther King Jr. as speakers. I attended the conference and joined them for lunch before they spoke. Dorothy was wearing an old, black dress with white pearls tangled with the chain of a religious medal, her white hair arranged in braids around her head. I was not surprised that she was overweight because, as she once dryly observed, only the rich can afford to be thin. Twice during lunch she appeared to have lost her speaking notes, thinking someone had taken them. In any case, she did not refer to her notes when she spoke that afternoon, just giving "witness," as was her usual style.

Over lunch I mentioned that I had used *The Long Loneliness* in a parish discussion group. The group, I told her, found it a "sad book." She responded, firmly, "It is not a sad book. We must go after perfection, as St. Paul says, not as having it but always tending toward it."

A significant part of her personal striving toward perfection was giving up the bohemian life of Greenwich Village and the intellectual circles she once frequented, as well as painfully and only gradually separating from the father of their daughter Tamar because of his refusal to accept her Catholic beliefs, which included the baptism of their child.

The diaries of Dorothy Day were published in 2008 under the title *The Duty of Delight*. Robert Ellsberg, the editor, said he chose this title because Dorothy was fond of it. He quotes her as follows:

> Today I thought of a title for my book, *The Duty of Delight*, as a sequel to *The Long Loneliness*. I was thinking of how, as one gets older, we are tempted to sadness, knowing life as it is here on earth, the suffering, the Cross. And how we must overcome it daily, growing in love, and the joy which goes with loving.[5]

Editing the diaries, Ellsberg said how impressed he was that this woman of immense activity maintained what he termed "the intense discipline of her spiritual and sacramental life."

> She attended daily Mass, which usually meant rising at dawn. She prayed the monastic hours from the breviary. . . . She devoted time each day to meditating on scripture, saying the rosary or other spiritual exercises. None of this is particularly remarkable. And yet the matter-of-fact recital of such habits underscores the fact that her daily life was spent in continuous reference to God. As she writes, "Without the sacraments of the church, I certainly do not think that I could go on."[6]

Psychoanalyst Robert Coles has written much about Dorothy Day, whom he met as a young medical student at the house of hospitality on Manhattan's lower east side. Coles found her engaged in a deep, seemingly interminable conversation with a woman who was obviously inebriated. When would this absurd conversation end? "Finally," Coles recalls,

> silence fell upon the room. Dorothy Day asked the woman if she would mind an interruption. She got up and came over to me. She said, "Are you waiting to talk with one of us?" One of us: with those three words she had cut through layers of self-importance, a lifetime of bourgeois privilege and scraped the hard bone of pride. . . . With those words, so quietly and politely spoken, she had indirectly told me what the Catholic Worker Movement is all about and what she herself was like.[7]

Simone Weil provocatively once wrote, by way of expressing her attraction to it, that Catholicism is a religion of slaves. This humble, hospitable feature of Catholicism also intrigued both Dorothy Day and Edith Stein. They saw very humble folk, poorly dressed, entering Catholic churches through the day to say their prayers and feeling at home there.

Dorothy Day's spiritual autobiography, *The Long Loneliness,* ends with these powerful summary statements of her most deeply held beliefs.

> We cannot love God unless we love each other, and to love we must know each other. We know

Him in the breaking of the bread, and we know each other in the breaking of the bread, and we are not alone anymore. Heaven is a banquet and life is a banquet, too, even with a crust, where there is companionship.

We have all known the long loneliness and we have learned that the only solution is love and that love comes with community.

It all happened while we sat there talking, and it is still going on.[8]

Dialogue Points for a Conversation with the Eucharistic Lord

1. Think of Jesus and Dorothy Day being totally indiscriminate in their friendships and table companions. Ask Jesus to help you be a welcoming presence to all you meet and to see and identify discrimination wherever you encounter it.

2. At the end of her life, Dorothy Day experienced discouragement and sadness through all the injustices and sorrows of the world, just as she had many times before. Even so, she pledged to accept "the duty of delight." Ask the Lord to give you delight in all you do, even the most challenging tasks.

Prayer

O holy banquet in which Christ is received,
his passion is recalled,
our souls are filled with grace,
and the pledge of future glory is given to us.

O Lord, I am not worthy
That Thou should come to me,
But say the word of comfort
And my spirit healed shall be.

O Sacrament most holy,
O Sacrament divine,
All praise and all thanksgiving
Be every moment thine.

FOURTH
WORD

"Father, into your hands
I commend my spirit."
(Lk 23:46)

❧◈❧◈❧◈❧◈❧◈❧

Pondering the Word

In the Gospel According to St. Luke, the very last words of Jesus before dying are taken from the thirty-first psalm. Like Psalm 22, it is a psalm of lament.

> Take pity on me, O God,
> for I am in trouble.
> Vexation is gnawing away my eyes,
> my soul deep within me.
> For my life is worn out with sorrow,
> and my years with sighs.
> My strength gives way under my misery,
> and my bones are all wasted away. (Ps 31:9–10)

But the verse from this psalm that Luke has Jesus utter upon the cross is not one of despair but one of hope and confidence in God's faithful love for him, "Father, into your hands I commend my spirit" (Lk 23:46), which continues, "by you I have been redeemed" (Ps 31:5).

In praying this psalm, Jesus accepts his human weakness and vulnerability in the face of the overwhelming forces arrayed against him. He turns to the Father who alone can rescue him, the One the psalm calls "my rock."

> Be for me a rock-fortress,
> a fortified citadel to save me.
> You are my rock, my rampart:
> true to your name, lead me and guide me. (Ps 31:2–3)

Wallace Stevens (1879–1955) at the age of seventy wrote one of his most analyzed poems, "The Rock." Stevens's poetry wrestles with the problem of belief in an unbelieving age; "The Rock" is a supreme example of this. In it, just a few years before his death, Stevens chronicles the disappointments of his life, especially his loveless marriage to the beautiful Elsie, whom he once described as growing cold at his slightest touch. Stevens was raised in a religious home and was well aware of the biblical image of the rock as a symbol for God. In the poem, however, the rock becomes reality itself, bare and comfortless. Looking back on his early love it all seems now "an invention," an act of desperation, an illusion like green leaves trying to cover the rock's barrenness.

The poet finds tranquility in creating poems as "icons" of blessedness that express his desires and celebrate nature's abundance. In this way, he says in the poem, he "makes meanings of the rock."[1]

Wallace Stevens once memorably quipped, "Disillusion is the last illusion." His aim as a poet and as a person was to see reality, the rock, unadorned, without illusion or disillusion. But still with his mind's eye he could create the poems that bring illumination and become "night's hymn of the rock" without distortion or wishful thinking.[2]

Stevens expressed a desire to encounter a "fresh spiritual," a spirituality that is suited to an age of skepticism. He achieves this through his poems, icons of beauty, and the unquenchable expression of the soul in its desire for God. The poetry provides a starting point, "the gate to the enclosure."[3]

Jesus upon the cross without flinching faced cruel reality and yet was able to utter a prayer of beauty, illumination, and trust. He thus went beyond illusion and disillusion with life and was able to see his God as his rock.

Like Wallace Stevens, Emily Dickinson (1830–1886) in her poetry questioned the traditional consolations of the Christian faith. Like him she also poetically rediscovered for herself the power and the truth behind them. In the following poem on the theological virtue of hope, Dickinson images hope in birdlike form as the Holy Spirit is often portrayed. The bird of hope comes uninvited as an unexpected divine gift—its melody beyond the capacity of human words to describe. That melody never ceases—in gale and storm, in cold, or in vast extremities like the sea. Hope, she writes, is pure gift, unearned and for that reason all the more precious.

"Hope" is the thing with feathers—
That perches in the soul—
And sings the tune without the words—
And never stops—at all—
And sweetest—in the Gale—is heard—
And sore must be the storm—
That could abash the little Bird
That kept so many warm—

I've heard it in the chillest land—
And on the strangest Sea—
Yet, never, in Extremity,
It asked a crumb—of Me.[4]

Dialogue Points for a Conversation with the Eucharistic Lord

1. Hope is defined as a "virtue," that is, a strength of soul in the face of adversity. It is also described as a "theological" virtue because its force and power come not from ourselves but from God, specifically God's fidelity to his promises. Ask Jesus to help you to be a more hope-filled person, especially in those circumstances when you must rely on God alone.

2. A third theological virtue, along with hope and charity, is faith. Faith is rightly described as unshakable trust, for faith's opposite is not doubt but fear. "Why are you so frightened?" Jesus challenged the apostles in the midst of the storm at sea (Mk 4:40). Say to the Lord with the apostles, "Lord, increase our faith" (Lk 17:5).

Blessed John XXIII

(1881–1963)

Behind the genial smile and peasant simplicity of Angelo Roncalli, Pope John XXIII, was a closely guarded secret, his soul and the constant soul work in which he was so seriously engaged all his life. From 1895, when he was fourteen, until 1962, a few months before his death at eighty-one—a span of almost seventy years—he kept a daily journal to which he later gave the title *Il Giornale dell' Anima* (*The Journal of a Soul*). In it he was constantly talking with God and placing himself at God's disposal.

His life was a public one and far removed from the contemplative sphere: secretary to his bishop in Bergamo, spiritual director at the local seminary, president for Italy of missionary societies, apostolic delegate in the Near East, papal nuncio to France, patriarch of Venice, and pope.

Upon becoming a bishop, he took special thought in selecting his episcopal motto. "Insert in my coat of arms," he writes in *The Journal*, "the words *Oboedientia et pax* (Obedience and peace). . . . These words are in a way my own history and my life."[5]

In 1959, during a retreat at the Vatican after his election as pope, John XXIII expanded upon his vision of his life as one of obedience to God in all things.

> Since the Lord chose me, unworthy as I am, for this great service, I feel I have no longer any special ties in this life, no family, no earthly country or nation, nor any particular preferences with regard to studies or projects, even good ones. Now, more than ever, I see myself only as the humble and unworthy "servant of God and servant of the servants of God." The whole world is my family. This sense of belonging to everyone must give character and vigor to my mind, my heart and my actions.
>
> This vision, this feeling of belonging to the whole world, will give a new impulse to my constant and continual daily prayer: the Breviary, Holy Mass, the whole rosary and my faithful visits to Jesus in the tabernacle, all varied and ritual forms of close and trustful union with Jesus.
>
> The experience of this first year gives me light and strength in my efforts to straighten, to reform, and tactfully and patiently to make improvements in everything. . . . I feel I am under obedience in all things and I have noticed that this disposition, in great things and in small, gives me, unworthy as I am, a strength of daring simplicity. . . .
>
> Above all one must always be ready for the Lord's surprise moves, for although he treats his loved ones well, he generally likes to test them with all sorts of trials such as bodily infirmities,

bitterness of soul and sometimes opposition
so powerful as to transform and wear out the
life of the servant of God . . . making it a real
martyrdom.[6]

Pope John loved to repeat what he called "the mystery of my life," the words of St. Gregory Nazianzen,
"The will of God is our peace."[7] In a homily on the feast
of Pentecost, 1962, he inserted this prayer: "Let everything in us be on a grand scale: the search for truth and
the devotion to it, readiness for self-sacrifice, even to the
cross and death."[8]

The Journal of a Soul is a day-by-day chronicle of someone's search for holiness in all life's small details. There
is nothing dramatic and startling to be found in them.
The great spiritual breakthrough for Angelo Roncalli is
an entry recorded early on, in 1903, when he was still a
seminarian.

Practical experience has now convinced me of
this: the concept of holiness which I had formed
and applied to myself was mistaken. In every
one of my actions, and in the little failings of
which I was immediately aware, I used to call
in mind the image of some saint whom I had set
myself to imitate down to the smallest particular, as a painter makes an exact copy of a picture
by Raphael. I used to say to myself: in this case
St. Aloysius would have done so and so, or: he
would not do this or that. However it turned
out that I was never able to achieve what I had
thought I could do, and this worried me. The
method was wrong. From the saints I must take

the substance, not the accidents, of their virtues. I am no St. Aloysius, nor must I seek holiness in his particular way, but according to the requirements of my own nature, my own character, and the different conditions of my life. I must not be the dry, bloodless reproduction of a model, however perfect. God desires us to follow the examples of the saints by absorbing the vital sap of their virtues and turning it into our life-blood, adapting it to our own individual capacities and particular circumstances. If St. Aloysius had been as I am, he would have become holy in a different way.[9]

John XXIII, unlike his predecessor Pope Pius XII, was by background a member of the peasantry, not the nobility. Many had written him off early on as a "chatterbox" and without depth or talent. He was relegated for years to the hinterlands of papal diplomacy before being summoned to be nuncio to France after World War II. Charles De Gaulle had demanded that Pope Pius XII purge the hierarchy of all the bishops who had collaborated with the Vichy regime. Roncalli, who was very much on the sidelines during World War II, seemed a good choice to do the job and his appointment might even have been the Vatican's reprimand of De Gaulle by sending him this unknown diplomat. John knew his election as pope at the age of seventy-seven made it appear the cardinals wanted only a transitional figure after the long pontificate of Pius XII. He confided to his journal,

When on 28 October, 1958, the cardinals of the Holy Roman Church chose me to assume the supreme responsibility of ruling the universal flock of Jesus Christ, at seventy-seven years of age, everyone was convinced that I would be a provisional and transitional pope. Yet, here I am already on the eve of the fourth year of my pontificate, with an immense program of work in front of me to be carried out before the eyes of the whole world, which is watching and waiting.[10]

John's spirituality of obedience to the will of God as the grounding for our peace is very much in keeping with Jesus' words from the cross, "Father, into your hands I commend my spirit."

Dialogue Points for a Conversation with the Eucharistic Lord

1. "Obedience and peace" was Blessed John XXIII's lifelong motto by which he lived his life. It is a variation on the familiar maxim "In God's will is our peace." Ask the Lord to help you follow his plan for your life.

2. Blessed John XXIII prayed, "Let everything in us be on the grand scale: the search for truth and the devotion to it, readiness for self-sacrifice, even to the cross and death." Let the Eucharist serve as a model to you of a life lived on the grand scale.

Prayer

God our Father, the contradiction of the cross proclaims your infinite wisdom. Help us to see that the glory of your Son is revealed in the suffering he freely accepted. Give us faith to claim as our only glory the cross of our Lord Jesus Christ, who lives and reigns with you and the Holy Spirit, one God, forever and ever. Amen.

Lord Jesus Christ, you gave us the Eucharist as a memorial of your suffering and death. May our worship of this sacrament of your body and blood help us experience the salvation you have won for us and the peace of the kingdom where you live with the Father and the Holy Spirit, one God, for ever and ever. Amen.

FIFTH WORD

"Woman, this is your son. Son,
this is your mother."
(Jn 19:27)

St. John's gospel, where these words are found, is the gospel of "signs"—meaning that the events of Jesus' life are presented as steeped in mystery and meaning. Just from this perspective, it is clear that, when Jesus from the cross entrusts his mother to the beloved disciple standing by and the beloved disciple to his mother, he is not concerned primarily about their domestic arrangements. At his death Jesus is designating his mother as the mother of every Christian, indeed of all humanity. Reaching back even further in salvation history, Jesus is declaring Mary to be the new Eve, "the mother of all those who live" (Gn 3:20).

John provides the clue to this deeper meaning when he has Jesus refer to his mother as "woman." Eve was the first to be called "woman" (Gn 2:23). Only one other time in the Gospel of John does Jesus refer to his mother as "woman," and that is at the wedding feast of Cana, which "was the first of Jesus' signs by which he revealed his glory, and his disciples believed in him" (Jn 2:11).

The account of the country wedding in a village of Galilee takes up only twelve verses in John, but every detail of it is meant to communicate the salvific role of the Son of God in human affairs.

We are told that among the guests at the wedding "the mother of Jesus was there, and Jesus and his disciples " (Jn 2:1). Mary's role is deliberately prominent not just because she is the first guest named but also because she is the first to speak and to notice, "They have no wine" (Jn 2:3). From her maternal concern she is the one who calls to Jesus' attention what would have been a

huge embarrassment in the culture of the Middle East, a
failure of hospitality toward your guests.

Jesus responds, "Woman, what do you want from
me? My hour has not yet come" (Jn 2:4). The word "hour"
has very special meaning. The hour of any creature of
God is the moment prepared by God when it manifests
the very purpose for its being, its deepest identity. A tree
bearing fruit is its "hour." A woman giving birth to a
child experiences "that her hour has come." Jesus' hour,
the moment of his glorification in the Gospel of John, is
his death upon the cross.

But Jesus does acquiesce to his mother's tacit request,
superabundantly. The six empty stone water jars, at his
instruction, are filled "to the brim" with water, each
containing twenty or thirty gallons. The water is trans-
formed into not just wine but wine of the finest vintage.
The guests have never tasted such excellent wine, nor
could they consume all the wine Jesus, the hidden host,
provided. Later, Jesus will feed the starving multitudes
with so much bread that there "were twelve large baskets
with scraps left over" (Jn 6:13). We begin to understand
how the Gospel of John could refer to the wedding at
Cana as the first of his signs, a manifestation of the glory
of God, when the disciples first believed in him. The wedding guests found themselves suddenly in paradise, to
which Mary, the new Eve, and Christ, the new Adam,
had introduced them.

The miracle of the wine at Cana and the miracle of
the bread for the multitudes have obvious eucharistic
overtones. The guests bask in the presence of Jesus who

provides them with a foretaste of what it will be like to dine in the kingdom of God.

And thus it was when Jesus' mission from the Father was about to be accomplished upon the cross, "from that hour the disciple took her into his home." Mary had heard years before, when her child was just an infant, that he would be "a sign of contradiction" and that her own soul would be pierced by a sword because of it (Lk 2:34–35). Now Mary knew the full meaning of Simeon's prophesy.

The Book of Revelation is believed to owe its origin to the Johannine community. It arose as a book of comfort for a church under severe persecution. Its heavenly visions were intended to assure them of their final victory over their foes by the power of God. In that book a woman appears robed with the sun, standing upon the moon and with a crown of twelve stars. She gives birth to a son who is lifted up to God and with her heel she crushes the serpent's head (Rev 12). Unlike the first Eve, who was deceived by the serpent's wiles, the new Eve resists him and reopens the gates of paradise.

The passion narrative in the Gospel According to John concludes with one of the soldiers, after Jesus had died, piercing his side with a lance. "And immediately there came out blood and water" (Jn 19:27). This is a deliberate allusion to the Book of Genesis where God made Adam fall into a deep sleep and while he was asleep fashioned Eve from a rib taken from his side (Gn 2:21–22). From the side of Jesus the new Adam, in the sleep of death, God fashions the Church represented by blood and water: the sacraments of the Eucharist and Baptism.

In the First Letter of John, we read,

> This is he who came by water and blood, Jesus
> Christ, not with water alone, but with water and
> blood, and it is the Spirit that bears witness, for
> the Spirit is Truth. So there are three witnesses,
> the Spirit, water and blood; and the three of
> them coincide. (Jn 5:6–8)

In his meditation upon these words, Pope Benedict
XVI calls attention to the emphasis upon the actual physi-
cal body of Jesus that bled real blood upon the cross.
Christianity, he continues, is not a philosophy of thoughts
and of ideas but a religion of flesh and blood, sacrifice
and sacrament.[1]

Dialogue Points for a Conversation with the Eucharistic Lord

1. Picture yourself beneath the cross with Mary, Jesus' mother.
    Jesus notices you and says to you, "Behold, this is your
    mother." How can you thank him for this final personal
    gift of his own mother as your own?

2. Ask Mary to help you develop within yourself what Pope
    Benedict XVI has called "the heart that sees," the heart that
    notices things, as did Mary at Cana of Galilee, saving the
    young couple's embarrassment.

Blessed John Paul II

(1920–2005)

As the second millennium of the birth of Christ drew near, Pope John Paul II issued a reflection upon the Mother of the Redeemer. Citing the Second Vatican Council, he recalls that the Church in the course of history "proceeds along the path already trodden by the Virgin Mary who 'advanced in her pilgrimage of faith and loyally persevered in her union with her son unto the cross.'"[2] There, he says, "Mary's motherhood . . . is a gift, a gift which Christ himself makes personally to every individual."[3]

Karol Wojtyla's life was characterized by devotion to the Mother of God who, he believed, saved him when he lost his own mother at the age of eight. The words of Jesus "This is your mother" (Jn 19:27) had personal significance for him; he once called them "the origin of all Marian devotion."[4] Throughout his life the Rosary was an important prayer for John Paul.

> From my youthful years this prayer has held an important place in my spiritual life. . . . The Rosary has accompanied me in moments of joy and in moments of difficulty. To it I have entrusted any number of concerns; in it I have always found comfort. . . . On October 29, 1978, scarcely

two weeks after my election to the See of Peter, I frankly admitted, "The Rosary is my favorite prayer."[5]

During all the years of his pontificate, Pope John Paul invited anyone who wished to join him in a public recitation of the Rosary on Saturday evenings in the Vatican. He personally wrote a new set of meditations, the "Luminous Mysteries," concentrating on Jesus' public life, to accompany its prayers.

If you stand in front of St. Peter's Basilica in Rome, you will notice on the right a mosaic portrait of Jesus and Mary placed there by John Paul. His personal coat of arms sets aside traditional symbols of family and nation and consists simply of the Cross of Christ with one bar elongated over a large letter *M*: Mary at the foot of the cross. His episcopal motto beneath it reads "Totus tuus," which is a short rendition of the prayer, "I am totally yours, dear Jesus, through Mary your mother."

During the Wojtyla years, the pope's private chapel in his apartment was adorned above the altar with the image of Our Lady of Czestochowa, patroness of Poland and focus of its religious identity. The original icon, piously believed to have been painted by St. Luke, is housed in a shrine on the mountain of Jasna Gora where, on August 15, people from all over Poland gather in pilgrimage. The faces of the Virgin and Child are darkened with the patina of the ages, and the face of the Virgin shows a slash done by an enemy of religion that has never been repaired.

On the Feast of Our Lady of Fatima, May 13, 1981, during a Wednesday public audience in St. Peter's

Square, the Turkish terrorist Ali Agca fired a shot at the pope, nearly killing him. A year later, Pope John Paul traveled to Portugal to place the bullet in a crown for Our Lady of Fatima, attributing to her his survival from this attack.

Some who have known him have called John Paul II a mystic. Let me cite one personal experience I had that confirms it for me. I was asked to visit the apartment in the Vatican of Cardinal Andrzej Deskur, a close personal friend of the pope going back many years to their earlier lives in Poland. Deskur, whom I met that day for the first time, showed the effects of a crippling stroke that struck him just three days before the election of his friend Wojtyla as pope. The new pope interpreted this event as a mystical offering by his friend for the success of his pontificate.

Before our meeting, I spent some time in the cardinal's private chapel. When we sat down together afterward, he asked me if I had noticed anything unusual about his chapel and I responded that I did not. Then he told me the remarkable story of how his friend, coming from Poland for meetings in Rome, would stay with him in this apartment and how he discovered that his friend was spending entire nights lying on the chapel floor in prayer before the Blessed Sacrament. It was then that Deskur decided to remove the traditional Italian tile floor from the chapel and replace it with wood, "so my friend would not catch a cold."

Before being ordained a priest, Karol Wojtyla worked in a stone quarry. When I met him and talked with him over the years, he appeared to me to be a man of stone.

He had to be to live through not one but two totalitarian
regimes in his homeland and survive. In one of his poems
called "The Quarry," he wrote,

> Hands are a landscape. When they split, the pain
> of their sores
> surges free as a stream.
> But no thought of pain—
> no grandeur in pain alone.
> For his grandeur he does not know how to name.[6]

John Paul II saw as his mission in life to point out the
grandeur of being a human person, and the amazement
for that grandeur, he once wrote, is the Gospel.

Dialogue Points for Conversation with the Eucharistic Lord

1. Feel the comfort of Mary standing with you through all
   the challenges of your life. Let her maternal care for you
   relieve you of the undue burdens you may have placed
   upon yourself.

2. The Gospel is "good news" because it is a message not of
   condemnation but of our greatness, dignity, and worth, as
   well as of our personal uniqueness. Ask the Lord to help
   you appreciate more your personal grandeur in the eyes
   of God.

Prayer

THE MAGNIFICAT

My soul proclaims the greatness of the Lord,
my spirit rejoices in God, my Savior
for he has looked with favor on his lowly servant.
From this day all generations will call me blessed:
the Almighty has done great things for me,
and holy is his Name.
He has mercy on those who fear him
in every generation.
He has shown the strength of his arm,
he has scattered the proud in their conceit.
He has cast down the mighty from their thrones,
and has lifted up the lowly.
He has filled the hungry with good things,
and the rich he has sent away empty.
He has come to the help of his servant Israel
for he has remembered his promise of mercy,
the promise he made to our fathers,
to Abraham and his children for ever.

SIXTH
WORD

"I thirst." (Jn 19:28)

The death of Jesus is steeped in prayer. Now, at the very end, Jesus expresses his longing for God in words taken from the psalms.

> God, you are my God, I pine for you
> my heart thirsts for you,
> my body longs for you,
> as a land parched, dreary and waterless.
> Thus have I gazed on you in the sanctuary,
> seeing your power and your glory. (Ps 63:1–2)

> As the deer yearns for running streams
> so I yearn for you my God.
> I thirst for God, the living God;
> when shall I go to see the face of God?
> (Ps 43:1–2)

Maybe it is hard for us today to understand how someone could have such a deep desire for God that the experience could be described as like living in a desert without water. In a secular world this basic human need and desire for God is often covered up by our pursuit of other pleasures that obscure our deepest self and its fundamental orientation toward God. Jesus now stripped of everything and soon of life itself shifts his whole attention to God as the one reality on which he can count.

One day I made the Stations of the Cross along the actual route Jesus followed in Jerusalem toward Calvary. Then as now this path goes through the bazaar, the ancient shopping arcade, which still exists. Recall how in the scriptures a man who came in from the country to shop, Simon of Cyrene, was enlisted to help Jesus carry his cross (Mk 15:21). I remember how odd it felt to be kneeling on the stone pavement of a public street while people were shopping and bargaining all around me. Odd, but right, because I was seeking something that could not be purchased in any shopping center, and for that reason it felt just right.

In his *Confessions*, St. Augustine describes his student days in just these terms.

> There was a hunger within me from a lack of that inner food, which is yourself, my God. Yet by that hunger I did not hunger, but was without desire for incorruptible food, not because I was already filled with it, but because the more empty I was, the more distaste I had for it.[1]

In a direct reference to Psalm 69, the Gospel of John relates that a sponge of wine on a hyssop stick was placed on Jesus' lips. "To eat they give me poison, to drink vinegar when I was thirsty" (Ps 69:21). The mention of hyssop is significant. Hyssop was used to sprinkle the blood of the Passover lambs. We are to understand that Jesus, whose death in John was occurring at the very moment the lambs were being sacrificed in the Temple, is now the Lamb of God who takes away the sin of the world.

Now in his death Jesus himself becomes the source of living water through the Holy Spirit, for all who believe in him.

> Let anyone who is thirsty come to me!
> Let anyone who believes in me come and drink!

As scripture says, "From his heart shall flow
streams of living water." (Jn 7:37)

Later in life, after his conversion, St. Augustine
reflected back on his earlier life and his misplaced desires.
At last he realized that his thirst was for nothing else
than God.

> Late have I loved you, O Beauty so ancient and
> so new, late have I loved you! Behold you were
> within me, while I was outside: it was there that
> I sought you, and a deformed creature, rushed
> headlong upon these things of beauty which
> you have made. You were with me, but I was
> not with you. They kept me from you, those fair
> things which, if they were not in you, would not
> exist at all. You have called to me, and have cried
> out, and have shattered my deafness. You have
> blazed forth with light, and have shone upon
> me, and you have put my blindness to flight!
> You have sent forth fragrance, and I have drawn
> in my breath, and I pant after you. I have tasted
> you, and I hunger and thirst after you. You have
> touched me, and I have burned for your peace.[2]

Dialogue Points for a Conversation
with the Eucharistic Lord

1. St. Augustine discovered the source of his unhappiness
   was that he was "outside" himself, seeking his pleasures
   outside rather than inside where God resided within him.
   "I was outside myself, you were inside." The struggle to

remain, despite the many external pressures, inside your-self, is great. Ask Jesus to help you stay in touch with who you are.

2. Some religions like Buddhism see happiness as extin-guishing all personal desires. Christianity rather sees in our deepest desires our true self and God as the deepest desire we have. Ask God to help you seek him more and more as the source of your greatest personal fulfillment.

WITNESS:

Blessed Teresa of Calcutta

(1910–1997)

Mother Teresa recalled that it was on a train journey to Darjeeling, on September 10, 1946, that she received a second vocation within religious life, "a vocation to give up even Loreto where I was very happy and to go out in the streets to serve the poorest of the poor."[3] In 1928 she had left her home in Albania to join the Sisters of Loreto in Ireland who, at her request, assigned her to teach in India. She felt an overwhelming desire not just to teach the poor in school and then send them home but also to go live among them and experience herself the poverty in which they lived. September 10 is observed as "Inspiration Day," the true beginning of the Missionaries of Charity Mother Teresa was eventually allowed to found.

The mystical experience on the train placed her on Calvary with Jesus at the very moment he cried out "I thirst." She explained it this way to the Missionaries of Charity:

> "I thirst," Jesus said on the cross when Jesus was deprived of every consolation, dying in absolute poverty, left alone, despised and broken in body and soul. He spoke of his thirst—not for water— but for love, for sacrifice.

Jesus is God: therefore, his love, his thirst is
infinite. Our aim is to quench this infinite thirst
of a God made man. Just like the adoring angels
in heaven ceaselessly sing the praises of God, so
the Sisters, using the four vows of absolute poverty, chastity, obedience and charity towards the
poor, ceaselessly quench the thirsting God by
their love and of the love of the souls they bring
to him.[4]

Mother Teresa once summarized her life this way: "By
blood, I am an Albanian. By citizenship, an Indian. By
faith I am a Catholic nun. I belong entirely to the heart of
Jesus." I was present in Rome on October 19, 2005, when
Mother Teresa was beatified by her friend Pope John Paul
II. Her cause for sainthood had been introduced only two
years after her death. The square of St. Peter's was filled
to overflowing with people, many of them the homeless
whom Mother Teresa had befriended. At that time, the
Vatican had its own homeless shelter, thanks to Mother
Teresa. She had asked the pope if she might establish
one within the tiny area of the Vatican, and he assented,
provided she could find a location. She chose a site, but it
was rejected by the bureaucracy; they said it blocked an
emergency escape route from the Paul VI audience hall.
Not deterred, she had a plaque made and asked the pope
to bless it so she could place it at the site she had selected.
He did so, and the matter of the shelter's location was
closed. It bears the name *Domus Mariae*, House of Mary.

In his homily on the day of her beatification, Pope
John Paul alluded to the dark nights of the soul that

Mother Teresa endured during much of her life. Yet, he said,

> in her darkest hours she clung even more tenaciously to prayer before the Blessed Sacrament. This harsh spiritual trial led her to identify herself more and more closely with those whom she served each day, feeling their pain and, at times, even their rejection. She was fond of repeating that the greatest poverty is to be unwanted, to have no one to take care of you.[5]

For many it was startling to learn in Mother Teresa's posthumously published diaries that she lived much of her life in what she described as "terrible darkness." In one entry she writes, "If I ever become a saint, I will surely be one of darkness. I will continually be absent from heaven, to light the light of those in the darkness on earth."[6] In a letter to Jesus she once confided, "In my soul I feel just that terrible pain of loss—of God not wanting me—of God not being God—of God not really existing. What do I labor for? If there be no God—there can be no soul. If there is no soul, then Jesus you are not true. Heaven, what emptiness."[7]

As I reflected upon this prolonged depression that she expresses, my first reaction was that it was the result of her voluntary and prolonged exposure to so much human misery and suffering. She realized, as she often said, that she could help a few, but this did not solve the problem of poverty and injustice. "God does not expect us to be successful," she once offered in explanation, "only to be faithful." Faithful, yes, but at what personal cost?

It was at this point that I decided to reread the spiritual journal of St. Thérèse of Lisieux (1873–1897) after whom Mother Teresa was named. Her *Story of a Soul*, written in the last years of her short life, uses images that have their exact counterpart in Mother Teresa's diaries. I then realized a psychological explanation of Mother Teresa's "darkness" was inadequate to grasp the spiritual purification that St. Thérèse had propounded in almost identical language.

Like Mother Teresa, St. Thérèse had great ambitions for her life. She wanted to be a missionary, even within the confines of a cloister. She felt dejected that she could not as a woman become a priest but felt comfort when she read in St. Paul's First Letter to the Corinthians that the greatest vocation is "love." "Yes, I have found my place in the Church! My vocation is love!"[8]

St. Thérèse also experienced huge sorrows. Her mother died when she was four. Her father was clinically depressed. Her "second mother," her older sister Pauline, left the family to become a Carmelite. Her darkest entries in her journal come when she is suffering from tuberculosis, which would take her life.

Each in her own way, Teresa of Calcutta and Thérèse of Lisieux experienced the existential anguish of Jesus' cry from the cross, "I thirst."

During World Youth Days in 1997, Pope John Paul II declared St. Thérèse of Lisieux "Doctor of the Church" under the title of "Doctor of Grace." I was puzzled how the author of a single book, which was not really a book but a series of jottings, could be declared a Doctor of the Church. I was given an explanation by one who was involved in the process of conferring this title: in her life Thérèse had demonstrated that only grace could have personally saved her from complete breakdown under the overwhelming weight of what she was given to bear at such a young age. She herself described grace as "an elevator" that lifted her up when she could not possibly do so herself.

In an entry in her journal just a short time before her death, St. Thérèse wrote,

> I feel that my mission is about to begin, my mission of making others love God as I love him, my mission of teaching the little way to souls. If God answers my requests, my heaven will be spent on earth up until the end of the world. Yes, I want to spend heaven in doing good on earth.[9]

Many years later, Mother Teresa would say the same.

Proposing a shelter for the homeless in the Vatican was not an outlandish idea for Mother Teresa but part of her deepest conviction: that we must love the poor wherever we are.

> You will find Calcutta all over the world if you have the eyes to see. The streets of Calcutta lead to every man's door. I know that you may want to make a trip to Calcutta, but it is easy to love people far away. It is not always easy to love people who live beside us. What about the ones I dislike or look down upon?[10]

Dialogue Points for a Conversation with the Eucharistic Lord

1. Essential to personal holiness, according to Mother Teresa, is the practice of voluntary poverty, especially in a consumerist, materialist culture such as our own. She once commented, "Many people do not understand why we do not have washing machines, why we do not have fans, why we do not go to the cinema, why we do not go to parties. These are natural things and there is nothing wrong in having them. But for us we have chosen not to have [them]. . . . For us to be able to understand the poor, we must know what is actual poverty."[11] Ask Jesus in the Blessed Sacrament to help you look at your life and see what is superfluous so you may follow him without encumbrance.

2. Mother Teresa put into practice the "little way" of her namesake, St. Thérèse, that is, to practice the "small virtues" every day with everyone: be kind with your companions, be gentle and considerate with the poor, and be extremely kind with the sick. Think how you may do these humble things as part of your path to holiness.

Prayer

Community Prayer of the Missionaries of Charity

Dear Lord, the Great Healer, I kneel before you, since every perfect gift must come from you. I pray: give skill to my hands, clear vision to my mind, kindness and meekness to my heart. Give me singleness of purpose, strength to lift up a part of the burden of my suffering fellowmen, and a realization of the privilege that is mine. Take from my heart all guile and worldliness, that with the simple faith of a child, I may rely on you. Amen.

Reflect also on these words of Mother Teresa:

Our works of love are nothing but works of peace. Let us do them with greater love and efficiency—each one in her own or his own work in daily life: in your home, in your neighborhood. It is always the same Christ who says: "I was thirsty—not for water but for peace that satiates the passionate thirst of passion for war. I was naked—not for clothes, but for that beautiful dignity of men and women for their bodies. I was homeless—not for a shelter made of bricks but for a heart that understands, that covers, that loves (from the Beatification booklet, October 19, 2003).

SEVENTH WORD

"It is finished." (Jn 19:30)

⚜⚜⚜⚜⚜⚜⚜⚜

In John's gospel, Jesus is no mere victim of a cruel fate imposed unwillingly upon him by others. On the contrary, Jesus is totally in charge even to the end when he pronounces from the cross, "It is finished," meaning he has fulfilled the mission the Father has given him with total fidelity. Speaking as the Good Shepherd who lays down his life for his sheep, Jesus earlier declared, "The Father loves me because I lay down my life in order to take it up again. No one takes it from me: I lay it down of my own free will, and as I have power to lay it down, so I have power to take it up again, and this is the command I have received from my Father (Jn 10:16–18). Jesus marches through his passion in total command. There is in John no agony in the garden, no plea to the Father to take this cup away. Jesus freely lays down his life and then takes it up again. It is almost as if he has the power for his own resurrection. Having declared, "It is finished," meaning "It is fulfilled," Jesus then "gave up his spirit" (Jn 19:30).

John does not include in his Passion account the institution of the Eucharist. What he gives us instead is the washing of the feet of the apostles as an example that they must wash each other's feet. This is the very meaning of the Eucharist: the humble Christ stooping down to wash the feet, dirty from the dust of the road, as a symbol of his own self-giving for the salvation of the world.

> Jesus knew that the Father had put everything into his hands, and that he had come from God and was returning to God, and he got up from table, removed his outer garments and, taking

a towel, wrapped it round his waist; he then
poured water into a basin and began to wash the
disciples' feet and to wipe them with the tower
he was wearing. . . . "Do you understand . . .
what I have done to you? You call me Master and
Lord and rightly; so I am. If I then, the Lord and
Master, have washed your feet, you must wash
each other's feet. I have given you an example so
that you may copy what I have done to you." (Jn
13:3–5; 12–15)

The "hour" of Jesus has come, the moment of his
glory. The cross is not Jesus' moment of defeat but rather
his "lifting up": "When you have lifted up the Son of
man, then you will know that I am He" (Jn 8:28). Luke,
for reasons of his own theology, separates the death, resurrection, and ascension of the Lord over several days;
in John, all are part of a single event, Jesus' glorification.

Pope Benedict XVI in his book of reflections on Holy
Week speaks of the Passion of Christ in terms of "mystery," that is, a historical event that has such depths that
it reveals the very meaning of history. The historical event
conveys the darkness and irrationality of human sinfulness and at the same time the very holiness of God too
dazzling for our eyes.

Benedict's exegesis of the ascension is particularly
insightful. The disciples express "joy" at Jesus' departure,
he says, because Jesus has not really gone away. "'Ascension' does not mean departure into a remote region of
the cosmos but rather the continuing closeness that the
disciples experience so strongly that it becomes a source
of lasting joy."[1] Jesus has not gone away but comes to us

in a new form of closeness. Now he is no longer in one particular place in the world as he had been before: he is in every place. And the place he is most preeminently is in the Eucharist.

Dialogue Points for a Conversation with the Eucharistic Lord

1. Time is how we measure our nights and days, our lives—clock time, time on the calendar. But there is another measure of time's passing: God's time. In the scriptures it is called *kairos*. God thinks in epochs and ages, not in minutes and seconds. Jesus knew his God-determined hour was fulfilled when he died upon the cross for our sake. Ask Jesus to let you see your life on earth as a vocation from God given you to accomplish the particular mission only you could do in your uniqueness.

2. Jesus at the Last Supper gave us a personal example of humbly washing his disciples' feet to demonstrate that the Christian life is one of service. Ask God to help you to be more generous in your service of God and your neighbor.

WITNESS:
St. Margaret Mary Alacoque
(1647–1690)

B ernard Haring, the Redemptorist priest who sought to renew moral theology by delivering it from the categories of canon law to the language of the Gospel, wrote this regarding the devotion to the Sacred Heart of Jesus inspired by the life and witness of St. Margaret Mary Alacoque:

> History shows that devotion to the Sacred Heart of Jesus and a great love of the Eucharist are inseparable. Jesus, who gave us this memorial of his sacrificial and atoning love, is now present in the Eucharist to bestow on us the wonderful pledge of the love of his heart. It is especially in the Eucharist that he offers us an exchange of heart, conforming our hearts to his heart.[2]

The life of Margaret Mary Alacoque is a Cinderella story: the ugly princess oppressed by malicious relatives who marries the prince. It is also a narrative of mental illness and how through illness a person can discover the power of the Cross of Christ as salvation.

At the direction of her wise and benevolent Jesuit confessor, Margaret Mary confided in her autobiography all her spiritual experiences. She wished to have it destroyed at her death, but it was kept as a precious relic by her fellow religious of the Visitation whose order she had joined. The diary begins by noting the death of her father when she was very young and describing how her mother, being left with five children, had to be absent for long periods to support them. Her grandmother, aunt, and great aunt subjected her to what she described as a life of "continual martyrdom." Suffering from psychosomatic illnesses and sometimes unable to walk for as much as four years, she never left the house without the permission of these three persons. They continued to try to marry her off, but she felt drawn to the life of the convent despite her feelings of self-loathing. She often did violence to herself by her extreme penances.

After an unsuccessful period with the Ursulines, Margaret Mary entered the convent of the community founded by St. Francis de Sales and St. Jane Frances de Chantal, the Visitation nuns. There she was instructed to accept the humane and compassionate directives of her superiors and to follow the spirit of the rule.

One day, praying before the Blessed Sacrament, she felt herself "penetrated with the Divine Presence" and "abandoned [herself] to this Divine Spirit." She continues, "He made me repose for a long time upon His Sacred Breast where he disclosed to me the marvels of his love and in the inexplicable secrets of his Sacred Heart."

> My Divine Heart is so inflamed with love for men, and for you in particular that, being unable any longer to contain within itself the flames of its burning charity, it must needs spread them abroad by your means, and manifest itself to them in order to enrich them with the precious

treasures which I discover to you, and which
contain graces of sanctification and salvation
necessary to withdraw them from the abyss of
perdition. I have chosen you as an abyss of un-
worthiness and ignorance for the accomplish-
ment of this great design, in order that every
thing may be done by me.[3]

The private revelations of the Sacred Heart of Jesus to
Margaret Mary received official Church approbation. The
practice of setting aside the first Friday of every month
to the Sacred Heart as an assurance of salvation endured
for many years up to the present time. The mosque-like
church in Paris, Sacré Coeur, built as a national sign of
reparation for the crimes of World War I, remains as a
symbol of the power of her visions over France. But most
of all, the residual effects of the Catholic form of Calvin-
ism called Jansenism were finally erased. Margaret Mary
achieved for herself and for Catholicism the conviction
that we are loved by God even in our imperfection and
sinfulness.

The source of the spirituality that saved St. Margaret
Mary Alacoque is found in these words of Jesus:

Come to me, all you who labor and are over
burdened, and I will give you rest. Shoulder
my yoke and learn from me, for I am gentle and
humble of heart, and you will find rest for your
souls. Yes, my yoke is easy and my burden light.
(Mt 11:28–30)

This became the characteristic spirituality of the religious community she entered, which was founded by St. Francis de Sales.

Jesus is now everywhere with his merciful love, as St. Margaret Mary rediscovered for herself and for the world.

Dialogue Points for a Conversation with the Eucharistic Lord

1. Our society and culture constantly provide us with self-images that are often destructive: no one is ever smart enough, rich enough, or thin enough. Ask Jesus to help you appreciate even more deeply God's personal love for you.

2. Mental illness is pervasive in the world today, and yet mental illness can be our sharing in the Cross of Christ leading to our personal redemption. Bring all your stresses and pain to our crucified Lord.

Prayer

PRAYER OF ST. MARGARET MARY

My God, I offer you your well-beloved Son, in thanksgiving for all the benefits I have received from you. I offer him as my adoration, my petition, my oblation, and my resolutions; I offer him as my love and my all. Receive, O Eternal Father, this offering for whatever you will of me, since I have nothing to offer which is not unworthy of you, except Jesus, my Savior, whom you have given me with so much love. Amen.

St. Francis de Sales experienced liberation from his teenage depression by reciting this prayer no doubt familiar to St. Margaret Mary Alacoque.

THE MEMORARE

Remember, O most gracious Virgin Mary, that never was it known that anyone who fled to your protection, implored your help, or sought your intercession was left unaided. Inspired by this confidence, I fly unto you, O Virgin of virgins, my Mother. To you I come, before you I stand, sinful and sorrowful. O Mother of the Word Incarnate! Despise not my petitions, but in your mercy hear and answer me. Amen.

HYMNS
OF THE
PASSION
AND THE
EUCHARIST

O Salutaris Hostia

O saving Victim opening wide
The gate of heaven to man below.
Our foes press on from every side
Your aid supply, your strength bestow.

To your great name be endless praise,
Immortal Godhead, one in three,
O grant us endless length of days
In our true native land with you.

Down in adoration falling
Lo! the sacred Host we hail;
Lo! o'er ancient forms departing,
New rites of grace prevail;
Faith for all defects supplying
Where the feeble senses fail.

To the everlasting Father,
And the Son who reigns on high,
With the Holy Spirit proceeding
Forth from each eternally.
Be salvation, honor, blessing
Might and endless majesty.

Stabat Mater

At the cross her station keeping
Stood the mournful mother weeping,
Close to Jesus at the last.
Through her heart, his sorrow sharing,
All his bitter anguish bearing,
Now at length the sword had passed.

Oh, how sad and sore distressed
Was that mother highly blessed
Of the sole begotten One.
Christ above in torment hangs,
She beneath beholds the pangs
Of her dying glorious Son.

Is there one who would not weep,
'Whelmed in miseries so deep,
Christ's dear mother to behold?
Can the human heart refrain
From partaking in her pain,
In that mother's pain untold?

Bruised, derided, cursed, defiled,
She beheld her tender Child,
All with bloody scourges rent.
O sweet mother, font of love,
Touch my spirit from above,
Make my heart with yours accord.

Make me feel as you have felt;
Make my soul to glow and melt
With the love of Christ, my Lord.

Holy mother, pierce me through,
In my heart each wound renew
Of my Savior crucified.

Let me share with you this pain,
Who for all our sins was slain,
Who for me in torments died.
Let me mingle tears with you,
Mourning him who mourned for me,
All the days that I may live.

By the cross with you to stay,
There with you to weep and pray,
Is all I ask of you to give.
Virgin of virgins blest!
Listen to my fond request:
Let me share your grief divine.

Let me to my latest breath,
In my body bear the death
Of that dying Son of yours.
Wounded with his every wound,
Steep my soul till it has swooned
In his very blood away.

Christ, when you shall call me hence,
Be your mother my defense,
Be your cross my victory.
Amen.

Vexilla Regis

Abroad the regal banners fly,
Now shines the Cross's mystery;
Upon it Life did death endure,
And yet by death did life procure.

Who, wounded with a direful spear,
Did, purposely to wash us clear
From stain of sin, pour out a flood
Of precious water mixed with blood.

That which the Prophet-King of old
Hath in mysterious verse foretold,
Is not accomplished, whilst we see
God ruling nations from a Tree.

O lovely and refulgent Tree,
Adorned with purpled majesty;
Culled from a worthy stock to bear
Those Limbs which sanctified were.

Blest Tree whose happy branches bore
The wealth that did the world restore;
The beam that did the Body weigh
Which raised up hell's expected prey.

Hail, Cross, of hopes the most sublime!
Now in this mournful Passion time,

Improve religious souls in grace,
The sins of criminals efface.

Blessed Trinity, salvation's spring,
May every soul thy praises sing;
To those thou grantest conquest by
The holy Cross, rewards apply.

Pange lingua gloriosi

Sing, my tongue, the glorious battle
Sing the last, the dread affray;
O'er the Cross, the victor's trophy,
Sound the high triumphal lay:
Tell how Christ, the world's Redeemer,
As a Victim won the day.

God, his Maker sorely grieving
That the first-made Adam fell,
When he ate the fruit of sorrow,
Whose reward was death and hell,
Noted then this Wood, the ruin
Of the ancient wood to quell.

For the work of our salvation
Needs would have his order so,
And the multiform deceiver's
Art by art would overthrow,
And from thence would bring the med'cine
Whence the insult of the foe.

Wherefore, when the sacred fullness
Of the appointed time was come,
This world's Maker left his Father,
Sent the heav'nly mansion from,
And proceeded, God Incarnate,
Of the Virgin's holy womb.

Weeps the Infant in the manger
That in Bethlehem's stable stands;
And his limbs, the Virgin Mother

Doth compose in swaddling bands,
Meetly thus in linen folding
Of her God the feet and hands.

Thirty years among us dwelling,
His appointed time fulfilled,
Born for this he meets His Passion,
For that this he freely willed:
On the Cross the Lamb is lifted,
Where his life-blood shall be spilled.

He endured the nails, the spitting,
Vinegar, and spear, and reed;
From that holy Body broken
Blood and water forth proceed:

Earth, and stars, and sky, and ocean,
by that flood from stain are free.
Faithful Cross! above all other,
One and only noble Tree!
None in foliage, none in blossom,
None in fruit thy peers may be;
Sweetest Wood and sweetest Iron!
Sweetest Weight is hung on thee.

Bend thy boughs, O Tree of glory!
Thy relaxing sinews bend;
For awhile the ancient rigor,
That thy birth bestowed, suspend;
And the King of heavenly beauty
On they bosom gently tend!

Thou alone wast counted worthy
This world's ransom to uphold;

For a shipwrecked race preparing
Harbor, like the Ark of old;
With the sacred Blood anointed
From the smitten lamb that rolled.

To the Trinity be glory
Everlasting, as is meet;
Equal to the Father, equal
To the Son, and Paraclete:
Trinal Unity whose praises
All created things repeat.

Adoro te devote, latens Deitas

Hidden God, devoutly I adore thee,
Truly present underneath these veils:
All my heart subdues itself before thee,
Since it all before thee faints and fails.

Not to sight, or taste, or touch be credit,
Hearing only do we trust secure;
I believe, for God the Son hath said it—
Word of truth that ever shall endure.

On the Cross was veiled thy Godhead's splendor,
Here thy Manhood lieth hidden too;
Unto both alike my faith I render,
And, as sued the contrite thief, I sue.

Though I look not on thy wounds with Thomas,
Thee, my Lord and thee, my God I call:
Make me more and more believe thy promise,
Hope in thee, and love thee over all.

O Memorial of my Savior dying,
Living Bread, that givest life to man;
May my soul, its life from thee supplying,
Taste thy sweetness, as on earth it can.

Deign, O Jesus, Pelican of heaven,
Me, a sinner, in thy Blood to lave,
To a single drop of which is given
All the world from all its sin to save.

Contemplating, Lord, thy hidden presence,
Grant me what I thirst for and implore,
In the revelation of thy essence
to behold thy glory evermore.

Good Friday, 1613, Riding Westward

Let mans Soule be a Spheare, and then, in this,
The intelligence that moves, devotion is.
And as the other Spheares, by being growne
Subject to forraigne motions, lose their owne,
And being by others hurried every day,
Scarce in a yeare their naturall forme obey:
Pleasure or businesse, so our Soules admit
For their first mover, and are whirld by it.

Hence is't, that I am carryed towards the West
this day, when my Soules forme bends towards the
    East.
There I should see a Sunne, by rising set,
And by that setting endlesse day beget;
But that Christ on this Crosse, did rise and fall,
Sinne had eternally benighted all.
Yet dare I almost be glad, I do not see
that spectacle of too much weight for mee.

Who sees Gods face, that is selfe life, must dye;
What a death were it then to see God dye?
It made his owne Lieutenant Nature shrinke,
It made his footstoole crack, and the Sunne winke.
Could I behold those hands which span the Poles,
and tune all spheares at once, peirc'd with those
    holes?
Could I behold that endlesse height which is
Zenith to us, and our Antipodes,

Humbled below us? or that blood which is
the seat of all our Soules, if not of his,
Made durt of dust, or that flesh which was worne
By God, for his apparell, rag'd, and torne?
If on these things I durst not looke, durst I
Upon his miserable mother cast mine eye,
Who was Gods partner here, and furnish'd thus
Halfe of that Sacrifice, which ransom's us?

Though thse things, as I ride, be from mine yes,
They'are present yet unto my memory,
For that looks towards them; and thou look'st
    towards mee,
O Saviour, as thou hang'st upon the tree;
I turne my backe to thee, but to receive
Corrections, till thy mercies bid thee leave.
O thinke mee worth thine anger, punish mee,
Burne off my rusts, and my deformity,

Restore thine Image, so much, by that grace,
That thou may'st know mee, and I'll turne my face.

JOHN DONNE

NOTES

Introduction

1. John Paul II, *Ecclesia de Eucharistia*, encyclical letter, April 17, 2003, no. 1.

2. Ibid., 6.

3. Ibid., 10.

4. Ibid., 25.

5. Ibid.

6. *Teresa of Avila, St. Teresa of Avila: The Life,* trans. J. M. Cohen (Baltimore: Penguin, 1957), 63.

First Word

1. Although the *New Jerusalem Bible* uses the name "Yahweh" here and in other Psalms quoted in this book, following the 2008 Vatican directive and in deference to the Jewish practice, "God" is used in its place in this text.

2. Simone Weil, *Gateway to God* (Glasgow, Scotland: Collins, 1974), 48.

3. Ibid.

4. Cited by Robert Coles, *Simone Weil: A Modern Pilgrimage* (Woodstock, VT: Skylight Paths, 2001), 34–35.

5. Simon Weil, *The Simone Weil Reader,* ed. George A. Panichas (New York: McKay, 1977), xxviii.

6. Weil, *Gateway to God,* 154.

7. Coles, *Simone Weil,* 125.

8. Cited in Weil, *Simone Weil Reader,* 16.

9. Cited by John Hellman, *Simone Weil: An Introduction to Her Thought* (Philadelphia: Fortress, 1982), 76.

10. Simone Weil, "The Father's Silence," in *Simone Weil Reader*, 433.

11. Weil, *Simone Weil Reader*, 4–5.

12. Weil, "The Father's Silence," *Simone Weil Reader*, 435.

Second Word

1. Hannah Arendt, *The Human Condition* (Chicago: University of Chicago Press, 1958), 238.

2. Ibid., 240.

3. Ibid., 241–42.

4. Paul Hamans, *Edith Stein and Companions on the Way to Auschwitz* (San Francisco: Ignatius, 2010), 81.

5. Edith Stein, *Self Portrait in Letters*, trans. Josephine Koeppel, O.C., vol. 5 (Washington, DC: OCS, 1993), 295.

6. Ibid., 291.

7. Ibid., 128.

8. Ibid., 145–46.

9. Ibid., 309.

10. *Edith Stein Carries the Light of* Christ *during the Horror of Auschwitz*, Gino Concetti, O.F.M., *L'Osservatore Romano English*, no. 31, August 5, 2009, 9.

11. Benedict XVI, "General Audience, May 31, 2006," *L'Osservatore Romano English*, June 7, 2006, 11.

12. Cited in Dianne Marie Traflet, *Saint Edith Stein: A Spiritual Portrait* (Boston: Pauline, 2008), 22.

13. Eric Metaxas, *Bonhoeffer: Pastor, Martyr, Phophet, Spy* (Nashville, TN: Thomas Nelson), 278.

Third Word

1. Raymond E. Brown, *The Death of the Messiah*, vol. 2 (New York: Doubleday, 1993), 1013.

2. See William D. Miller, *A Harsh and Dreadful Love: Dorothy Day and the Catholic Worker Movement* (Garden City, NY: Image, 1974), 108–9.

3. Benedict XVI, *Caritas in veritate*, June 29, 2009, no. 39.

4. Cited by Jim Forest, *Love Is the Measure* (Maryknoll, NY: Orbis, 1994), 142.

5. Dorothy Day, *The Duty of Delight: The Diaries of Dorothy Day*, ed. Robert Ellsberg (Milwaukee, WI: Marquette University Press, 2008), foreword.

6. Ibid., xvii.

7. Robert Coles, *Dorothy Day: A Radical Devotion* (Reading, MA: Addison-Wesley, 1987), xviii.

8. Dorothy Day, *The Long Loneliness* (Garden City, NY: Image, 1959), 276–77.

Fourth Word

1. Wallace Stevens, *Collected Poetry and Prose* (New York: Library of America, 1997), 445–47.

2. Ibid.

3. Ibid.

4. Emily Dickinson, *The Complete Poems of Emily Dickinson*, ed. Thomas H. Johnson (Boston: Little Brown, 1960), 254.

5. John XXIII, *The Journal of a Soul* (New York: McGraw-Hill, 1965), 206.

6. Ibid., 298–99.

7. Ibid., 326.

8. Ibid., 397.

9. Ibid., 106–7.

10. Ibid., 303.

Fifth Word

1. Joseph Ratzinger, *Jesus of Nazareth: Holy Week* (San Francisco: Ignatius, 2011), 225–26.

2. John Paul II, *Redemptoris Mater*, encyclical letter, March 25, 1987, no. 2.

3. Ibid., no. 45.

4. Ibid., no. 6.

5. John Paul II, *Rosarium Virginis Mariae*, apostolic letter (Boston: Pauline, 2002), no. 2.

6. John Paul II, *The Place Within: The Poetry of Pope John Paul II*, trans. Jerzy Peterkiewicz (New York: Random House, 1979), 64–65.

Sixth Word

1. Augustine, *Confessions* (New York: Doubleday, 1960), 3:1.

2. Ibid., 5:27.

3. Mother Teresa, *Come Be My Light*, ed. Brian Kolodiejchuk, M.C. (New York: Doubleday, 2007), 39–40.

4. Ibid., 41.

5. George Weigel, *The End and the Beginning: Pope John Paul II; The Victory of Freedom, the Last Years, the Legacy* (New York: Doubleday, 2010), 347.

6. Mother Teresa, *Come Be My Light*, 1.

7. Ibid., 193.

8. Thérèse of Lisieux, *Story of a Soul*, trans. John Clarke, O.C.D. (Washington, DC: ICA Publications, 1996), 194.

9. Ibid., 263.

10. Mother Teresa, *No Greater Love* (New York: New World Library, 1997), 159.

11. Cited in Susan Conroy, *Mother Teresa's Lessons of Love and Secrets of Sanctity* (Huntington, IN: Our Sunday Visitor, 2003), 151–52.

Seventh Word

1. Ratzinger, *Jesus of Nazareth*, 281.

2. Bernard Haring, C.S.S.R., *The Sacred Heart of Jesus: Yesterday, Today and Forever* (Liguori, MO: Liguori Press, 1999), 27.

3. Margaret Mary Alacoque, *The Autobiography* (Rockford, IL: Tan, 1986), 67.

Monsignor Charles M. Murphy is the director of the permanent diaconate for the Diocese of Portland, Maine. He is the author of a number of scholarly articles and several books, including *The Spirituality of Fasting*, *At Home on the Earth*, *Wallace Stevens: A Spiritual Poet in a Secular Age*, and *Belonging to God*. Murphy is the former academic dean and rector of the Pontifical North American College in Rome and served as part of the editorial group working in Italy under Cardinal Ratzinger on the third draft of the *Catechism of the Catholic Church*, which became the fourth and final version.

Murphy serves as consultant to the United States Conference of Catholic Bishops committee on catechetics, reviewing materials for conformity with the Catechism. He served as chair of the editorial committee that produced the pastoral letter on environmental issues by the Bishops of the Boston Province and as a consultant to the USCCB for their statement on global warming. He has been the pastor of four parishes in Maine and has served his diocese in ecumenical and educational capacities. Murphy holds a doctorate in sacred theology from the Gregorian University, a master's degree in education from Harvard University, and a bachelor's degree in classics from the College of the Holy Cross.

Founded in 1865, Ave Maria Press,
a ministry of the Congregation of
Holy Cross, is a Catholic publishing
company that serves the spiritual and
formative needs of the Church and its
schools, institutions, and ministers;
Christian individuals and families; and
others seeking spiritual nourishment.

For a complete listing of titles from

Ave Maria Press

Sorin Books

Forest of Peace

Christian Classics

visit www.avemariapress.com

ave maria press® / Notre Dame, IN 46556
A Ministry of the United States Province of Holy Cross